The Guideposts Christmas Treasury

The Editors of Guideposts

Phoenix Press

WALKER AND COMPANY
New York

To the memory of Pat Ayers of
Guideposts, who suggested this project
to us at Walker and Company.

**Large Print Edition published by arrange-
ment with Guideposts Associates, Inc.**

Copyright © 1986 by Guideposts Associates,
Inc.

First Large Print Edition, 1986
Walker and Company

Would you like to be on our Large Print
mailing list?

Please send your name and address to:

Beth Walker
Walker and Company
720 Fifth Avenue
New York, NY 10019

Library of Congress Cataloging-in-Publication Data

The Guideposts Christmas treasury.

   1. Christmas—Meditations.   2. Christmas—Literary
collections.   3. Large type books.   I. Guideposts
(Pawling, N.Y.)
BV45.G83   1986   242'.33   86-20454
ISBN 0-8027-2565-1

Printed in the United States of America

See page 122 for Credits.

Table of Contents

INTRODUCTION

This book was created out of deep gratitude for the greatest Christmas gift of all—the Christ child. Born in a stable almost 2,000 years ago, He returns to our hearts each Christmas, bringing precious gifts of the spirit which are ours to cherish and enjoy.

Here then, with thanks to the One who makes it possible, is an outpouring of those gifts from the **Guideposts** family of writers and editors.

We think Christmas is a time when families should be together. Whether you live alone or with loved ones, we pray that you will join us as we prepare our hearts and homes to receive the Gift of Christmas.

THE EDITORS

PART I
Advent—
Preparing for Christmas

AN ADVENT PRAYER

Father,

Prepare our hearts for Your
    coming. Quiet the
stirrings within. Calm the
    busyness without.
Renew us with Your Spirit.

We are ready, Lord—ready for
    Christmas . . .
Ready to hear the cries of our
    injured neighbor.
Ready to extend our hands to a
    fallen brother.
Ready to sit with a hurting friend.
Ready to comfort a grieving child.
Ready for You.

With open hearts, we receive the
    Christ Child
into our lives today.

                                    Amen.

                        TERRI CASTILLO

THE SECRET OF HAPPY GIVING

Catherine Marshall

Christmas—the time for giving and receiving gifts—is here again. Pondering the commercialism that seems to characterize this holiday season, I began to wonder if the Bible had anything to say about gifts and giving that might be helpful.

When I turned to it, one portion of the Sermon on the Mount seemed especially pertinent. If we stand in the temple, Jesus said, about to offer a gift to God, and suddenly remember that a friend has a grudge or resentment against us, we are to postpone giving the gift. We are to go and be reconciled to our friend, then come back and offer our gift to God; only then

will He receive our offering and bless us. Relationships are primary, He seems to be saying; gifts secondary.

When the relationship **is** right, how precious the gift becomes. I remember the autumn my father spent many weeks making my Christmas gift—a doll bed, dresser and china cupboard. To this day I can shut my eyes and see that miniature furniture, painted white and with glass knobs on the drawers and cupboard doors. But surely the reason I remember it so fondly and in such detail is that the gift spoke of the father-daughter relationship behind it. The handmade furniture said, "I love you; you are important to me—important enough to be worth any amount of my time and my very best effort."

Such gifts are a spontaneous expression of unselfish love. But can we say the same for all the gifts that we give at Christmas time? Isn't it true that sometimes we use the device of a gift to conceal or paper over a flawed relationship? Or—even more common—isn't our attitude sometimes: "I'm giving you this gift because I feel I must (because you expect it, or because you're likely to give me something and I must reciprocate, or because I

really don't know how to get out of this bleak and joyless exchange)"?

Perhaps this Christmas all of us should examine our gift lists to see if any of our giving falls into that category. If so, why not try the happy experiment of applying Jesus' priority to the situation: **First** be reconciled to thy brother, **then** offer thy gift.

We could try it with just one person. As we look down our list, is there anyone for whom we invariably have trouble finding a gift? Is there someone we resent shopping for? Anyone with whom we feel uncomfortable, no matter what we give them? Those can be clues to relationships that need mending.

Once we have selected the person, the next step is to devote time each day to thinking and praying about the relationship. Is the person a neighbor or a co-worker? Perhaps we've never really focused on him as a human being. We have not cared enough even to seek out his needs and preferences. The answer here could be a lunch date, a visit to his home, half an hour of real conversation. Does some old, never-acknowledged resentment lie between us and some member of the family? Healing could take the form of a letter, a face-to-face meeting or simply an interior act of confession.

Whatever the relationship we choose to work on and whatever the steps we take to improve it, we should wait until we are satisfied that it is as close to the one God intended as we can make it. Only then should we proceed with the secondary matter of selecting a gift. The price tag will not matter, as our gift does what all true gifts do—it reflects transparent love.

When we give in that spirit, we are truly making ready for Christmas when Love itself comes down to earth. Then with the Wise Men, we too can kneel at His crib and give thanks for the greatest gift of all.

A CHRISTMAS TREE— FOR THE BIRDS, TOO!
June Masters Bacher

The little birds of the Holy Land were once remembered at Christmas by sheaves of grain placed on housetops, so that the sparrows could share the joyous season.

Later, according to legend, children in Stockholm gathered packages from the festive tree beside the great stone fireplace inside, while the birds collected their sweetmeats from the evergreen outside. So began the practice of the birds' Christmas tree, a charming custom you and your family may enjoy reviving.

If you have any tree in your yard, it would look inviting looped with colorful come-and-eat-me garlands for hungry little birds. Or what about the artificial tree in the attic you have planned to discard? Give it to the birds! Be sure to "plant" it right in front of a much-used window, and your act of goodness is sure to bring a flock of rewards.

To prepare a delectable treat for the

birds, purchase suet at the market. Prepare a basic syrup of one cup of sugar and three cups of water. Allow it to boil several minutes before adding the suet. After the mixture cools (but before it jells) add rolled oats, chopped nuts, stale bread cubes, yellow cornmeal, and peanut butter (amount can vary). Roll the mixture into ball-shapes and package them individually in little squares cut from open-mesh sacks such as dry onions come in. Tie with a bit of bright ribbon and hang among the branches as you would on the family tree.

Hang crackers, stale cookies, and doughnuts, too. Fill favor cups with cracked corn, dry peas, or assorted nuts (unsalted) and suspend them here and there. Thread needles with colored yarn and string table variety cheeses, cranberries, and popcorn. Loop the tree with these nutritious chains and get ready for the birds' reaction.

Some birds like melons. If **your** birds are among them, cut melon rinds into chunks and include them on the menu. String dried currants and raisins and let the strands dangle for "easy picking."

Remember that some birds are salad lovers! For these birds no meal is complete without apple slices, banana wedges, whole plums, cabbage wedges, and lettuce leaves. Your guest list will grow as the menu varies.

Sprinkle rice on the ground to resemble snow (if you live in a warm climate); make it prepared cereal if nature sends snow on her own. Be generous with sunflower seed, acorns, and sesame seed in order to accommodate both large and small birds. And, last, would you believe that some birds like dog biscuits?

And remember that birds get thirsty even in winter. Place little tins of water here and there around the tree. In cold climates, you will need to change it often if the temperature is low.

A custom revived can add to your Christmas pleasure this year. Think of the fun you and your family will have decorating the tree. But most important of all you may very well be saving the lives of many little songbirds who will reward you with their music, come Spring. What a wonderful way to say "Merry Christmas!" to God's little creatures.

O LITTLE TOWN

Nancy Schraffenberger

Many years passed before I was old enough to understand why my young parents had worked such long hours in the chilly dimness of the carriage barn, oiling leather and rusty hinges, sanding splintered wood, waxing dull metal. But I know now that they were drawn by a sense of the rising magic of Christmas Eve, to make a necessary journey . . .

On December 24th, in the Depression year 1937, a vast white blanket, thick and rumpled, covered the fields in the Mohawk Valley. Across the frozen river from the farmhouse where my grandmother and I stood at a window, the lights of the very small village glistened like a handful of stars scattered in the snow.

"It's a fine clear night," my grandmother said. "The folks over there won't have any trouble getting to the midnight service." I looked up into her face and saw her faded-blue eyes focused longingly on the little village church steeple that rose above the rooftops far across the drifted snow on the other side of the river,

pointing to the sky in the shape of praying hands.

She sighed, then let the curtain fall over the window and we turned back to the glow of the kerosene lamps lighting the parlor. "It's time to get the creche ready, Nancy," she said, lifting down a wooden box from the top of the piano. "Soon Baby Jesus will be here."

My parents and I were staying with my grandmother in the old family homestead that winter when I was four. Instead of closing the house and renting a room in the city for the cold months, as she normally did, Grandma had invited us to move in with her—three miles out in the country—until my father could find work and we could afford to live on our own.

The isolated house was an antique— 150 years old, with no electricity and only the most primitive heating and plumbing.

But we were cozy there. We ate, worked and socialized in the big warm kitchen and slept near Franklin stoves in the back parlor and dining room. The root cellar was heaped high, and rows of gleaming Mason jars displayed jewel-like contents—emerald peas, ruby tomatoes, golden peaches and such—canned the previous summer. Occasionally, people brought my father mechanical repairs to do; my mother and grandmother had a kind of cottage industry, making braided rugs that were sold by a city department store.

Our only lack, really, was transportation. My grandmother's automobile was permanently parked in the barn alongside broken-down wagons and carriages; there was no money for gasoline. During mild weather we could row across the river to the village on the opposite shore to attend

10

church and buy necessities at the general store. But when the snow fell and the river froze and the razor-edged winds came slicing down the valley, only my father made that trip, by foot, and only to replenish vital food supplies.

It was not getting to church services that was a real hardship for Grandma. After her husband died and, one by one, her six children moved away, the congregation had become her family. There she had taught Sunday school, played the organ, laundered the altar cloths; she had brought home-made biscuits and preserves for new mothers, home-grown flowers for the shut-in and bereaved.

By Christmas Eve, Grandma hadn't seen her church or her church family for almost three months. Though she longed to welcome Jesus in God's House, she knew this was not possible. Now she and I carefully laid out the manger scene on the parlor mantelpiece. While we worked, my parents came in from the mysterious business that had occupied them off and on for the past few weeks. We ate an early supper and then gathered around Grandma at the piano to sing carols. Afterward I remember the feeling of closeness and love as I was passed from lap to

lap while the grown-ups took turns reading the Christmas scriptures in Matthew and Luke. At some point I must have fallen asleep and been put to bed. And some time after that my parents must have told Grandma about their Christmas gift to her.

My first knowledge of it was my mother's urgent whisper, "Wake up, Nancy, there's a surprise." She tugged my leggings and heavy sweater on over my flannel nightgown and wrapped me in my quilt. Then my father came in and picked me up, a fat patchwork bundle,

and carried me out the front door. Waiting in front of the porch steps was a box sleigh filled with straw and hitched to it a pair of huge mules as tall as houses. My grandmother was already seated in the back, wreathed in a tapestry of quilts, regal as a queen. My father tucked me in next to her and she drew me close. Spellbound, I watched him help my mother up on the bench seat and climb up beside her.

"All set?" he asked, looking over his shoulder. "Gee up, Buck, gee up, Bright!" He cracked the reins smartly on the mules' backs and the great creatures set their hooves, then leaned into their harnesses. With a lurch, the sleigh moved forward, snow squeaking under its runners. It moved jerkily at first, then more smoothly as the mules settled into a stride. The cold air was like a sparkling

tonic I could taste. Above, the arching night sky was scribbled with silver constellations; the world around us was a darkened amphitheater filled with breathless, motionless waiting.

My father guided the sleigh around the rutted driveway to the back of the house, over the snow-covered garden and down the incline to the cove where we docked the rowboat in the summer. Then we were on the river ice, marble white and marble solid, the mules stepping securely, the harness bells jingling like a pocketful of coins.

"Grandma," I whispered, "where are we going?" I looked up into her face, as carved and keen as an old shepherd's.

She gazed back at me and in the crystalline moonlight I could see her eyes. They were starred with happiness.

"To Bethlehem," she said.

"CHRISTMAS CARD" FRIENDS

Laura Norman

Outside, the snow swirls under the street lights. Inside, it's warm and cozy as my family gathers around the empty dining room table.

Carefully, I place the thick telephone directory in the center of the table, close my eyes and flip to a page at random. Then, eyes still closed, I lift my pencil high in the air and bring it down on a name while the family cheers!

This is a yearly ritual that started six years ago when I found my Christmas list completed and cards left over.

The name and address picked from the telephone directory is copied on a Christmas card envelope. Now it is my daughter's turn to do the same, then the boys, and last, my husband. Tomorrow, I will put our return address in the left-hand corner, stamp these envelopes, and mail them.

The years have brought us many "Christmas card friends." There is the University student who had lived too far away to go home for Christmas; there is the shut-in I visit all year around, and there is the family who moved out of the

state soon after receiving our card, though we're now penpals.

Some of our cards are returned. A few we never hear from, but many people do respond and enrich our lives with their friendships.

13

I recall one day many years ago when I was frightened of my first day at a new school. My mother smiled and patted my shoulder. "There are no strangers in the world, honey," she said, "only people waiting to become friends." And what wonderful blessings "strangers" can be when they become your "Christmas card friends" all through the years.

GO, TELL IT ON THE MOUNTAIN

Down in a lowly manger
   the humble Christ was born,
And God sent us salvation
   that blessed Christmas morn.
Go, tell it on the mountain,
   over the hills and everywhere,
Go, tell it on the mountain
   that Jesus Christ is born.

SANTA LUCIA

Ann Lindholm

The thirteenth of December is known as Santa Lucia Day and begins the Swedish Christmas celebration. There are several legends concerning Lucia. One legend describes Lucia as a medieval Saint, clothed in a flowing white robe with a crown of light encircling her head, carrying food and drink to the hungry folk in the Swedish province of Varmland. Another legend originates on the island of Sicily, where a young girl about to be a bride gave her entire dowry to the poor and admitted to being a Christian. She was convicted of witchcraft and burned at the stake on December 13th, 304 A.D. Sometime later, she was declared a saint by the church.

Today at dawn, on December 13th, households throughout Sweden (and those with Swedish descendants, living elsewhere) are awakened by a Lucia. The eldest daughter, dressed in the traditional white robe with a crimson sash and wearing a crown of lighted candles, serves coffee and pastries to each member of the family as she sings **Santa Lucia.**

For our family this is a very special time. Our daughter awakens each of us with her song. We huddle together in one bedroom. The candles brighten the dark mid-winter morning as we enjoy our coffee and cardamom rolls. We try to sing Christmas carols with foggy and sleepy voices. Then we are silent—we see each other reflected by the candle glow and there is a warm, wonderful feeling of love. We ponder the beginning of another Christmas season, and the Christ Child's presence—with all His warmth and love and hope—becomes very real to each of us.

LONG, LONG AGO

AUTHOR UNKNOWN

Winds through the olive trees
Softly did blow,
Round little Bethlehem
Long, long ago.

Sheep on the hillside lay
Whiter than snow;
Shepherds were watching them
Long, long ago.

Then from the happy sky
Angels bent low,
Singing their songs of joy
Long, long ago.

For in a manger bed,
Cradled we know,
Christ came to Bethlehem
Long, long ago.

INTEGRATING THE FAMILY TREASURES

Ruth C. Ikerman

It was the first Christmas since the marriage of my young friend to a handsome father of two children. Since he had their custody, my friend became an Instant Mother.

I asked her how the holidays had been, and a frown crossed her usually attractive face. "I'm so glad Christmas is over," she told me, "but next year will be better."

"What happened?" I asked.

"It was all because we had two boxes of decorations for the tree. My husband brought out the ornaments the children had used in other years. Jeff and Helen made a dash for their favorites, and immediately put them on the tree limbs."

Meanwhile, she told me, she had been unpacking the ornaments she had collected in ten years as a career girl, expecting the children to enjoy using them as tree trimmings. The children had no feeling for the crystal icicles, the fragile ornaments with little figurines embedded between the clear substances. They cared not at all for the figures made of straw which my friend had secured in her travels to foreign countries.

"It was a real blow to my ego," she told me. "I expected them to like what I had enjoyed so much. They didn't even want me to put them on the tree with their toy drums, soldiers, fairies and dollies.

"Finally I sat down on the couch with the children and told them stories about each of my treasures. I offered them a chance to each choose the ones which they liked best.

"Reluctantly the children peeked into the box, and Jeff took out some ivory animals I bought in Alaska. Helen chose a wooden manger scene carved in Italy.

"I told them these figurines were theirs to keep as long as they lived. Shyly they gave me their thanks at first, and then followed them up with real hugs.

"The tree looked a little lopsided and

not as I had visualized it, but the longer I looked at it, the prettier their earlier ornaments looked to me. By the time Christmas was over it began to seem like a tree which belonged to all of us."

Wisely the Instant Mother had found one large box in which to put all the ornaments from the first tree they had shared.

"Next year we will just open the one box together." she told me.

I patted her on the shoulder and told her how much I admired her wisdom and her courage. By integrating the ornamental treasures, she had made unity out of what might have become a divided Christmas.

Wise in the ways of love and Christmas was my young friend, and rich in memories will be the children and their father in the newly established loving family circle.

HOW TO MAKE A JESUS TREE

Margaret Simpson of Eufaula, Oklahoma, doesn't know where she got the idea. All she knows is that when the time came to decorate the family's customary five-foot tree last Christmas, the same thought kept running through her mind, "It's Jesus's birthday. It's Jesus's birthday."

And suddenly she simply didn't want to use the same old Christmas decorations again. She wanted new ones, white ones, ones that reminded her of the Bible and of Jesus. Margaret's four-year-old granddaughter, Regan Leigh, liked the idea, too, and quite by chance suggested one of the first new decorations—a tiny loaf of bread from her dollhouse.

"Jesus is the bread of life!" Margaret exclaimed, and that led her to think of Regan Leigh's little toy lamps as the "lamp unto my feet," and a fleecy sheep as the "Lamb of God," and silver stars as "the bright and morning star." Soon the two of them were decorating the tree and talking about the Bible simultaneously.

Margaret went into shops in Eufaula and McAlester and Muskogee, asking for Christian-symbol decorations, but the shopkeepers would shake their heads; no one had asked for such a thing before. So she would go home and adapt some more, until by Christmas Eve her tree was shimmering with white lights (for purity), while white angels danced and butterflies (for the Resurrection) rested gently on the green branches. It was a wondrous sight, this thing she called her Jesus Tree, one that Margaret Simpson will recreate for her family this year, and in the years to come.

And who knows, someday Regan Leigh might be decorating a similar tree for her own grandchildren saying "Now these white doves are for the Holy Spirit, and these shiny staffs for the Good Shepherd, and these. . . ."

THE CHICKEN-POX CHRISTMAS

Janet Martin

Mother was harried before Christmas that year. I could not understand it. She kept complaining about not having enough time. Yet, to me, the hours stretched endlessly. Of course, I was home in bed, where I had been for a week with the chicken pox.

Bored, I scratched the pesky scabs that mottled my body. Mother fussed at me for scratching. She poured pink calamine lotion all over the sores. Then she hauled me out of bed, stripping the covers.

Because of the pox, Mother washed laundry every day. She pulled the heavy, wet sheets from the sink and loaded them into the wicker wash basket. Then, wiping a wisp of straggling, blond hair back from her forehead, she lifted the load and pushed open the screen door to the backyard.

Sometimes, as she stretched the sheets across the clothesline, she unhinged the pins from her mouth and called to Mrs. Darby next door. Mrs. Darby owned a dress shop in town. It was rather exclusive, Mother said, so we went only on sale days. I loved the shop. Wandering the aisles in Mother's footsteps, I rubbed my cheek against slippery, satin gowns. I fingered light laces and counted the pearls on beaded trims.

But today was not a sale day. It was simply a Saturday in December in Auburn, Alabama. The year was 1951.

I sat hugging my dolly on the back stoop, watching Mrs. Darby and Mother. I banged my seven-year-old knees together and listened to what the women were saying. Mother and Mrs. Darby talked about subjects that women always mentioned in whispers.

Mrs. Darby murmured that she and her daughter were "alienated," a word strange to me. Then Mother said that Daddy might go to Korea to war.

War. Suddenly it dawned on me that the reason Daddy wore blue all the time was because he was a soldier. But he was not like the ones in the newspaper. He carried books under his arm, and he walked each day to Auburn University, a few blocks down the street. Daddy was a teacher of cadets.

Once he said his uncle had given him his job. He laughed and winked at Mother.

"Uncle who?" I asked.

"Sam," he replied.

A button-eyed robin ran across the ground in front of me. He parted the pinestraw with his beak. I watched him; then I noticed that Mother had finished the wash. She stood with her hands under her apron, her head bent slightly. I strained to hear what she was saying to Mrs. Darby.

"Christmas just two weeks away," she sighed. "Santa Claus may not make it."

Santa not make it? A new horror. **What was wrong with him? Did Santa have the chicken pox?**

I flew off the stoop, ran to Mother and grabbed her skirt.

"What do you mean?" I shrieked.

"Oh, honey," Mother shrugged, "Santa doesn't have much money this year."

Mrs. Darby raised her ample frame upright. "There are two things I believe in," she puffed. "Time and faith. Time that works toward solutions, faith which speeds time along."

She squatted down beside me. "Let me tell you how it works, Janet," she said. "By Christmas morning, your chicken pox will be gone. Your dolly will have a new dress, and your Mother—well—she won't have to wash sheets every day."

"But what about your alienated daughter, Mrs. Darby?" I asked. "And what about Daddy? Will Daddy go to war?"

"We'll be leaving those things to God," she said. "In the meantime, we'll keep the faith. Now, you remember what I have said, will you?"

I closed my eyes and breathed in her words: time and faith. Then, I waited.

As the days rolled by, my scabs began to peel away, revealing new pink flesh underneath. Nights faded in and out. On Christmas Eve, Mother told me to lay my dolly beneath the Christmas tree. "It's a step of faith," she whispered.

All that night I tossed and turned. Excitement and hope intermingled in my sleep.

Christmas morning dawned cold, rainy. I slipped out of bed. My bare feet took the icy, wooden steps downstairs in twos. At the landing, I peeked over the banister into the living room below.

Mother and Daddy were sitting on the sofa sipping coffee. Underneath the tree was my dolly. She sat in splendor in a white satin bride dress. Tiny seed pearls roped her neckline; wide lace banded her hem. My parents looked tired, like they had been up late. But they were smiling. Daddy held a brown envelope in his hand.

"Hello, peanut," Daddy said, taking Dolly and me on his lap. "See, you kept the faith, didn't you?"

I looked triumphantly into Mother's face. "Mrs. Darby was right, Mom."

"Yes—time and faith," Mother nodded.

Several years would pass before I understood some things about that Christmas: the chicken pox went away by itself; Mother made my dolly's dress from a sample from Mrs. Darby's shop; Daddy had become eligible for discharge from the Armed Forces. My child's heart thought it was all God's doing. But then, maybe it was . . .

By the way, Mrs. Darby's daughter did not come home for Christmas that year. But judging from Mrs. Darby's powerful faith, I expect in time, on another Christmas, she did. After all, time and faith are all one needs to set God's power in motion. Even a child can have that . . . and not just on Christmas.

A PRE-CHRISTMAS PRAYER
Drue Duke

Lord, I went shopping today in my favorite store, the one that stocks that lovely china and vases and **bric-a-brac.** I was Christmas shopping for gifts for three friends.

But I came home empty-handed. Something in the store stopped me. Or, I should say—something that was **not** in the store stopped me.

All year, Lord, the statuette has been there on the shelf that holds the blown glass figures of birds and small animals and flowers. So many times I've admired it, the Good Shepherd carrying His lamb. Today it was gone, and I asked the clerk about it.

"We had to put it out of the way," she said. "We needed the space to display more Christmas merchandise."

I stood there, thinking about that, Lord. Put Jesus out of the way to make room for things that would be used to celebrate His birthday? That just didn't seem right.

Then I thought about my home—the big gaily decorated tree in the living room, the candles on the mantel, the wreath on the door, the poinsettia on the hall table. **The crèche packed in a box in the attic.** There hadn't seemed any place to put it!

I'm going up now to unpack it, Lord. And I will set it up in the most prominent room in the house. After all, what good are the candles or the tree or anything else—even life itself—without our Blessed Saviour's presence?

23

MY MERRY MONTH OF CHRISTMAS

Nita Schuh

Thanksgiving had been difficult enough—how would I ever make it through Christmas? I couldn't go running to family or friends again, or take a getaway cruise. No. The time had come to pick up the threads of losing Joe. Though his death had left me feeling empty, like a fresh mountain stream gone dry, somehow I knew I would have to find a way of restoring the joy to this holy season—without my husband. It pained me to think that his bubbly spirit would not be around to make the holidays full and complete. I had to accept that things could never again be the way they used to be. I had to let go of "us." I had to begin reaching forward—on my own.

December was here and Christmas was right around the corner. Nothing came to my mind. My spirits were heavy when I walked into the kitchen one morning. It was three weeks till Christmas, and I hadn't done a thing. Between sips of hot coffee, my eye suddenly caught my wall calendar hanging on the refrigerator door. The month of December peered back at me, the boxes glaringly empty until December 25th, circled in red. I felt ashamed.

I got up and took the calendar down, placing it on the table in front of me. "No more wasting time," I told myself. "**Right now** I will expectantly look forward to Christmas."

I picked up a pencil, and at the top of the calendar I wrote, "The Merry Month of Christmas," feeling anything but merry as I did so. Then, hoping for something inspirational to plan for, I began to idly fill in the blank squares: make cookies for Cousin Edie (89 years old, blind and in a nursing home); baby sit while Nancy, a friend's daughter, Christmas shops; address and mail Dad's cards; share holly and other greenery from my garden with Virginia, my apartment-dweller friend; have a tea for widowed friends in my

24

neighborhood, and so on.

I felt lighter. There was nothing spectacular, but before I knew it, nearly every date had been filled in and the margins of the calendar were full and overflowing with scribbled notes and ideas as well.

As the days unfolded and I began to actually do the things I had jotted down, an excitement for each day filled me in an unbelievable way. Soon my problem became, "How shall I get all of these things done?" I didn't want to leave **anyone** out! I could hardly believe that only a few weeks ago I had been so lonely I didn't even want to think about Christmas. Now I wished I had more time before Christmas arrived!

In the end, I did have plenty of time to do the things I had planned, and to enjoy the company of my friends. And when the month was over, I discovered it had, indeed, been the "Merry Month of Christmas" after all!

That was four years ago. Each year since, I've repeated my tradition in some form, and it has become more and more a time of happy anticipation as well. And I know Joe would have been proud of me. What is even more pleasing is that my little idea caught the imagination of others. Last year one friend called to tell me, "Remember when you celebrated all the month of December, Nita? Well, I'm doing that, too. . . ."

Maybe some of you might like to join us this year. If so, right now, take your December calendar and at the top of the page write, "The Merry Month of Christmas." Begin to fill in the squares with your own ideas . . . that's how it all began for me. The simple practice of making commitments brought rich rewards in learning to give—when I thought I had nothing—and in the end, made my Christmas full and complete.

A CHRISTMAS LIST

Marilyn Morgan Helleberg

"Ask," He said, "and you shall
  receive."
When you're nine years old, your
  heart can believe.
"Give me a doll that drinks and
  sleeps."
I asked, but oh, I didn't receive.

"Ask," He said, "and you shall
  receive."
I was young and in love, it was
  Christmas Eve.
"Give me the heart of that special
  boy."
I asked, but oh, I didn't receive.

"Ask," He said, "and you shall
  receive."
Money was scarce but I tried to
  believe.
"Give us enough for the gifts on
  our list."
I asked, but oh, I didn't receive.

"Ask," He said, "and you shall
  receive."
Sorting my values, I began to
  perceive.
"Give me Your Son. Let Him
  shine through me."
I asked, and lo, I began to
  receive . . .

More than I'd ever dared to
  believe
Treasures unmeasured, blessings
  undreamed,
All I'd asked or hoped to achieve.
"Ask," He said, "and you shall
  receive."

SURPRISE PACKAGES

Shirley Climo

For my mother, creating Christmas for three children during the depression years meant working within a strict budget. The gaily-wrapped gifts that awaited us beneath the Christmas tree were generally of a practical nature: flannel shirts and warm wool scarves, slippers and mittens needed to curb the chill of an Ohio winter. But we never felt the least deprived, for there were other presents, too. Big or little, bright or plain in their brown paper, these were the boxes that held our childhood dreams. They were empty.

With a dab of paste, a dash of paint, a handful of scraps, a heartful of determination, Mom transformed cardboard cartons into castles and doll houses, oatmeal boxes into doll cradles, apple crates into cupboards or cars. We were always delighted to find these "surprise packages" on Christmas morning, better by far than anything bought from a store.

Now, close to half a century later, I too, am recycling old boxes, remembering holidays past, and restoring some of my mother's Christmas spirit. For I've begun to understand what those "empty" boxes really held. They were filled to the top with love.

I begin my own Big Box Hunt just after Thanksgiving. This is the time that cardboard cartons really come into season, for merchants are busy unpacking holiday supplies and discarding boxes of all shapes and sizes. They're as happy to have the bulky containers off their hands as I am to lay hands on them.

Last Christmas, a stove carton became a candy house, straight out of "Hansel and Gretel." We pulled the end flaps of the box up and taped it to form a pitched roof. We painted it pink and adorned it with real, good-to-eat gingerbread boys and candy canes, affixed with powdered sugar frosting. We cut a door in one side, much too small for any grown-up, but just the right size to admit a four-year-old and friend.

Another year, we fashioned a similar carton into a puppet theatre. We covered the box with contact paper, attached a sequin-studded marquee to the top, and cut a proper stage opening into the side. Curtains sewed to brass rings hung from a wooden dowel, to slip open dramatically when the show began or draw hastily if

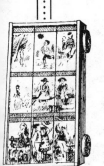

the star got the giggles.

"Good things come from small packages" is worth remembering, too. If there are little children on your Christmas list, look for little boxes. Smaller cartons are readily available at most stores, and the more collected the merrier. A dozen or so, taped shut and covered with stick-on paper make light, safe oversize building blocks. Perhaps others might wish to share one of my own childhood favorites: a pull-toy train. Mine was simply shoe boxes strung together, but each "gondola car" was boldly numbered from one to ten. As I transported favorite stuffed animals across the floor, I learned to count in the bargain.

For me, a special sort of magic goes into the making and the giving of Surprise Packages. Last Christmas, my seven-year-old grandchild said to me "Your presents aren't really surprises at all, Nana, because I always know what's going to be inside the box. ME!"

Perhaps, in a few decades, she'll discover that a lot of me was also tucked inside those empty boxes. ■

LOOK-AHEAD GIFTS

June Masters Bacher

Wouldn't it be nice if we kept Christmas alive after the carolers have gone, the Nativity scenes packed away, and the eaves stripped of their colored lights? This year why not resolve to keep alive the essence of the season by putting some year-round Spirit into your giving. It can be done—with a generous outlook at the world and an appreciative heart to the thoughtfulness of others.

Here are some look-ahead gifts that show your loved ones you want them to remember the gift of giving long after the holidays are past:

1. Plant daffodil bulbs in clay pots. Include a card telling the recipient how to take care of them when they bloom.
2. Bake a chocolate cake for a shut-in. Tuck in several copies of your recipe in case the person wishes to share a slice and "how-to."
3. Volunteer several hours of yard work at weeding time to a family member, a new neighbor, or a friend who shares flowers or vegetables in season.
4. Treat Dad to a free car wash on specified Saturdays.
5. Plan an old-fashioned "living room picnic" at least twice during the year (specify the dates for your family).
6. Treat Granddad to a baseball game—take along horehound and licorice and promise (yourself) to listen as he reminisces.
7. Let your children "sleep out" in the living room now and then. Supply sleeping bags and fill a thermos with hot chocolate. And let them giggle all night long.
8. Give your wife an umbrella—and offer to take a walk in the rain with her.

9. Volunteer a service you have never done—maybe never even attempted—for your church or community.

10. Give a large-print Bible to a visually-handicapped person and volunteer to take turns reading aloud.

Now, think up your own—but remember: Save the greatest gift of all for yourself. Add an "I love You" to every note and every farewell. You'll have your reward!

WE THREE KINGS OF ORIENT ARE

We three kings of Orient are;
Bearing gifts we traverse afar,
Field and fountain, moor and
    mountain,
Following yonder star.

Born a King on Bethlehem's
    plain,
Gold I bring to crown Him again,
King forever, ceasing never
Over us all to reign.

O star of wonder, star of night,
Star with royal beauty bright,
Westward leading still proceeding,
Guide us to Thy perfect light.
    Amen.

THE MIRACULOUS STAIRCASE

Arthur Gordon

On that cool December morning in 1878, sunlight lay like an amber rug across the dusty streets and adobe houses of Sante Fe. It glinted on the bright tile roof of the almost completed Chapel of Our Lady of Light and on the nearby windows of the convent school run by the Sisters of Loretto. Inside the convent, the Mother Superior looked up from her packing as a tap came on her door.

"It's **another** carpenter, Reverend Mother," said Sister Francis Louise, her round face apologetic. "I told him that you're leaving right away, that you haven't time to see him, but he says . . ."

"I know what he says," Mother Magdalene said, going on resolutely with her packing. "That he's heard about our problem with the new chapel. That he's the best carpenter in all of New Mexico. That he can build us a staircase to the choir loft despite the fact that the brilliant architect in Paris who drew the plans failed to leave any space for one. And

despite the fact that five master carpenters have already tried and failed. You're quite right, Sister; I don't have time to listen to that story again."

"But he seems such a nice man," said Sister Francis Louise wistfully, "and he's out there with his burro, and . . ."

"I'm sure," said Mother Magdalene with a smile, "that he's a charming man, and that his burro is a charming donkey. But there's sickness down at the Santo Domingo Pueblo, and it may be cholera. Sister Mary Helen and I are the only ones here who've had cholera. So we have to go. And you have to stay and run the school. And that's that!" Then she called, "Manuela!"

A young Indian girl of 12 or 13, black-haired and smiling, came in quietly on moccasined feet. She was a mute. She could hear and understand, but the Sisters had been unable to teach her to speak. The Mother Superior spoke to her gently: "Take my things down to the wagon, child. I'll be right there." And to Sister Francis Louise: "You'd better tell your carpenter friend to come back in two or three weeks. I'll see him then."

"Two or three weeks. Surely you'll be home for Christmas?"

"If it's the Lord's will, Sister. I hope so."

In the street, beyond the waiting wagon, Mother Magdalene could see the carpenter, a bearded man, strongly built and taller than most Mexicans, with dark eyes and a smiling, wind-burned face. Beside him, laden with tools and scraps of lumber, a small gray burro stood patiently. Manuela was stroking its nose, glancing shyly at its owner. "You'd better explain," said the Mother Superior, "that the child can hear him, but she can't speak."

Goodbyes were quick—the best kind when you leave a place you love. Southwest, then, along the dusty trail, the mountains purple with shadow, the Rio Grande a ribbon of green far off to the right. The pace was slow, but Mother Magdalene and Sister Mary Helen amused themselves by singing songs and telling Christmas stories as the sun marched up and down the sky. And their leathery driver listened and nodded.

Two days of this brought them to Santo Domingo Pueblo, where the sickness was not cholera after all, but measles, almost as deadly in an Indian village. And so they stayed, helping the harassed Father Se-bastian, visiting the dark adobe hovels where feverish brown children tossed and fierce Indian dogs showed their teeth.

At night they were bone-weary, but sometimes Mother Magdalene found time to talk to Father Sebastian about her plans for the dedication of the new chapel. It was to be in April; the Archbishop himself would be there. And it might have been dedicated sooner, were it not for this incredible business of a choir loft with no means of access—unless it were a ladder.

"I told the Bishop," said Mother Magdalene, "that it would be a mistake to have the plans drawn in Paris. If something went wrong, what could we do? But he wanted our chapel in Sante Fe patterned after the Sainte Chapelle in Paris, and whom am I to argue with Bishop Lamy? So the talented Monsieur Mouly designs a beautiful choir loft high up under the rose window, and no way to get to it."

"Perhaps," sighed Father Sebastian, "he had in mind a heavenly choir. The kind with wings."

"It's not funny," said Mother Magdalene a bit sharply. "I've prayed and prayed, but apparently there's no solution at all. There just isn't room on the chapel floor for the supports such a staircase needs."

The days passed, and with each passing day Christmas drew closer. Twice, horsemen on their way from Santa Fe to Albuquerque brought letters from Sister Francis Louise. All was well at the convent, but Mother Magdalene frowned over certain paragraphs. "The children are getting ready for Christmas," Sister Francis Louise wrote in her first letter. "Our little Manuela and the carpenter have become great friends. It's amazing how much he seems to know about us all. . . ."

And what, thought Mother Magdalene, is the carpenter still doing there?

The second letter also mentioned the carpenter. "Early every morning he comes with another load of lumber, and every night he goes away. When we ask him by what authority he does these things, he smiles and says nothing. We have tried to pay him for his work, but he will accept no pay. . . ."

Work? What work? Mother Magdalene wrinkled up her nose in exasperation. Had that softhearted Sister Francis Louise given the man permission to putter around in the new chapel? With firm and disapproving hand, the Mother Superior wrote a note ordering an end to all such unauthorized activities. She gave it to an Indian pottery-maker on his way to Sante Fe.

But that night the first snow fell, so thick and heavy that the Indian turned back. Next day at noon the sun shone again on a world glittering with diamonds. But Mother Magdalene knew that another snowfall might make it impossible for her to be home for Christmas. By now the sickness at Santo Domingo was subsiding. And so that afternoon they began the long ride back.

The snow did come again, making their slow progress even slower. It was late on Christmas Eve, close to midnight, when the tired horses plodded up to the convent door. But lamps still burned. Manuela flew down the steps, Sister Francis Louise close behind her. And chilled and weary though she was, Mother Magdalene sensed instantly an excitement, an electricity in the air that she could not understand.

Nor did she understand it when they led her, still in her heavy wraps, down the corridor, into the new, as-yet-unused chapel where a few candles burned.

"Look, Reverend Mother," breathed Sister Francis Louise. "Look!"

Like a curl of smoke the staircase rose before them, as insubstantial as a dream. Its base was on the chapel floor; its top rested against the choir loft. Nothing else supported it; it seemed to float on air. There were no banisters. Two complete spirals it made, the polished wood gleaming softly in the candlelight. "Thirty-three steps," whispered Sister Francis Louise. "One for each year in the life of Our Lord."

Mother Magdalene moved forward like a woman in a trance. She put her foot on the first step, then the second, then the third. There was not a tremor. She looked down, bewildered, at Manuela's ecstatic, upturned face. "But it's impossible! There wasn't time!"

"He finished yesterday," the Sister said. "He didn't come today. No one has seen him anywhere in Sante Fe. He's gone."

"But **who** was he? Don't you even know his **name?**"

The Sister shook her head, but now Manuela pushed forward, nodding emphatically. Her mouth opened; she took a deep, shuddering breath; she made a sound that was like a gasp in the stillness. The nuns stared at her, transfixed. She tried again. This time it was a syllable, followed by another. "Jo-se." She clutched the Mother Superior's arm and repeated the first word she had ever spoken. "Jose!"

Sister Francis Louise crossed herself. Mother Magdalene felt her heart contract. Jose—the Spanish word for Joseph. Joseph the Carpenter. Joseph the Master Woodworker of. . . .

"Jose!" Manuela's dark eyes were full of tears. "Jose!"

Silence, then, in the shadowy chapel. No one moved. Far away across the snow-silvered town Mother Magdalene heard a bell tolling midnight. She came down the stairs and took Manuela's hand. She felt uplifted by a great surge of wonder and gratitude and compassion and love. And she knew what it was. It was the spirit of Christmas. And it was upon them all.

A LASTING
CHRISTMAS

GARNETT ANN SCHULTZ

I keep a part of Christmas
For it helps to add a glow,
To the January darkness
And the February snow.
If March is cold and blustery
And though April brings us rain,
The peace and warmth of
   Christmas
With its happiness remain . . .

There's a beauty when it's
   Christmas
All the world is different then,
There's no place for petty hatred
In the hearts and minds of men.
That is why my heart is happy
And my mind can hold a dream,
For I keep a part of Christmas
With its peace and joy supreme.

Oh, God, we go through life so
    lonely, needing
  what other people can give us,
  yet ashamed to show that need.
And other people go through life
    so lonely,
  hungering for what it would be
  such a joy for us to give.
Dear God, please bring us
    together this Holy season,
  the people who need each
    other, who
can help each other, and would
    so enjoy each other.

                 MARJORIE HOLMES

PART II
The Joy of Christmas

"WHEN THEY SAW THE STAR . . ."

❦ ❦ ❦ Then Herod, when he had privily called the wise men, enquired of them diligently what time the star appeared. And he sent them to Bethlehem, and said, Go and search diligently for the young child; and when ye have found him, bring me word again, that I may come and worship him also. When they had heard the king, they departed; and lo, the star, which they saw in the east, went before them, till it came and stood over where the young child was. When they saw the star, they rejoiced with exceeding great joy . . .

MATTHEW 2:7-10

THE CHRISTMAS MIRACLE

Jean Bell Mosley

"What I need," Matt muttered to himself, "is a big fat miracle." He chopped away with all his twelve-year-old strength at the cedar he'd chosen for the Christmas tree.

It was up to him this year, what with Mom in the hospital and Dad there visiting her this Christmas Eve.

"I don't even know where the trimmings are, let alone how to get any lights," Matt continued, laying out his problem to the cold snowy world.

The tree fell with a soft swish. If it weren't for his younger brother and sister he wouldn't even fool with a tree or worry about lights for it. All he wanted was for Mom to be better and come home.

Matt slung the tree over his shoulder and hurried home. There was still the milking to do and the feeding. There'd have to be some sort of supper for Lance

and Lacy. It would be late before Dad got home from the hospital.

He wondered how the school Christmas program had gone that afternoon. He'd had to miss it in order to cut his tree.

He had some trouble getting the tree to stand up straight in the bucket of sand, but when it was done he placed it in front of a big window that overlooked the meadow. He wished he'd had time to find the baubles or make some. The kids were going to miss the promised lights but if he'd had some tinsel or paper chains maybe they wouldn't be so disappointed.

"Just one big fat miracle," Matt repeated. He closed the door to the front room and locked it. If he didn't let the kids see it until after dark, they wouldn't miss the decorations and tonight he might think of something.

After the milking, he threw down hay for the horse and fed the pig. Purple dusk was settling over the countryside. He could see a light on at the house and knew Lance and Lucy were home.

Glancing at the darkening sky he saw the evening star shining brightly and knew that soon the stars would be thick as daisies in a summer pasture. He wondered if that long-ago Bethlehem Star had looked like this one. Probably bigger and more shiny, he concluded.

"It was a miracle, I guess—that special Star. And we don't have such miracles any more," he told the chickens as he scattered their corn. "But I could sure use a great big fat one."

He removed his cap again, dusted it against his jeans and put it back on. It was a gesture he'd seen his Dad do lots of times. He didn't know why but, for him, it seemed to punctuate things—like a period indicating it was time to get on with something else.

After supper, when Lance and Lacy had helped tidy up, Matt got out the old Bible. Every year Dad did the reading, but he was man of the house now.

"And, lo, the angel of the Lord came upon them, and the glory of the Lord shone round about them and they were sore afraid," he read.

"How was it, Matt?" Lance demanded. "How did the angel come?"

"Well, I suppose he just came down out of the skies."

"Did you ever see anything like that, Matt?" Lance pressed.

"Naw, things like that don't happen anymore. It was sort of a—well, a miracle, I guess."

"Are we going to have a tree this year?" Lacy asked when he had put the Bible back on the shelf.

"We've got a tree," Matt replied, feeling proud. "And I'll let you have just one little peek tonight."

He opened the front room door and they tiptoed inside, closing the door behind them. The tree stood outlined against

the window. Matt heard a quick intake of breath in the darkness and waited.

"Oh, Matt, the lights!" Lacy exclaimed, clapping her little hands. "The lights! The lights! They're beautiful."

"What lights?" Matt asked.

"Nobody else ever had lights like these!" There was joy, awe, reverence in Lacy's voice.

"Where's the lights?" young Lance demanded.

"Come down here," Lacy said, pulling both their heads down on a level with her own. "See, at the very top and at the end of each limb—a star!"

It was true. The tree, silhouetted against the window, was alive with stars. They twinkled and sparkled through the branches with a very special one at the top.

"Oh, Matt, you did it," Lacy exclaimed, hugging and showering her brothers with kisses. "I knew we'd have lights!"

"I didn't do it," Matt said roughly, over the peculiar lump in his throat. "It's—it's—well, you know what I said about miracles not happening any more? That

just isn't so." He spoke slowly, feeling his way, something new happening inside him.

"It's just where you're looking at it from. That's it. That's what makes a miracle. It's just who's looking at it and where he's looking at it from."

He reached to remove his cap. It wasn't there. So he just smoothed his hair and smiled. It was time to get on with whatever came next, especially in a world where big fat miracles still happened.

WHY DON'T WE—AT CHRISTMAS?

It started years ago as an impromptu little Christmas ceremony in the home of the William T. Clawson family of Monkton, Maryland. The youngest of the three Clawson children, Curt, was in the service then, far away in Korea.

At midnight, as the clock ticked away the first seconds of the Lord's birthday, a candle was lighted, a candle so small that it would burn for only eight minutes. While the family gathered around its glow, the father, William Clawson, read the Christmas story from Luke, and then all the family prayed for Curt, and for one another, and for the whole of God's creation. In time those candlelit eight minutes became an annual ritual, the Clawsons' way of recognizing the truest meaning of Christmas.

The Clawson family tradition was adopted by their church, Monkton United Methodist. They prepared a Christmas card with a candle enclosed which says:

ON CHRISTMAS EVE

If everyone lit just one little candle, what a bright world this would be.

If everyone stopped for a few minutes to remember why we celebrate Christmas, what a significant holiday it would be.

If everyone offered just one little prayer for peace on earth, good will to all men, what a more compassionate world this would be.

MRS. PINE'S HAPPIEST CHRISTMAS

Robert Juhren

Every year, Mrs. Pine felt just a touch of guilt about taking a part-time job for the holidays. She didn't really need the money and felt she might be depriving some needy person of a job.

However, with no family of her own to shop for, she relished the work, the suggesting, the showing, the excited deliberations to choose just the right gift. And she loved the holiday decorations, the twinkling lights, even the irritable customers. To Mrs. Pine it was a glorious whirl of color, warmth and anticipation.

This year, Mrs. Pine turned down the usual offer from Fowler's Department Store, and took instead a job at a small toy store. It was owned by an elderly man named Mr. Miller who ran the shop single-handedly except at Christmas. Mrs. Pine was his only clerk.

On the Monday after Thanksgiving, she reported for work. As Mr. Miller showed her around the cluttered shop, she began to wish she had gone back to Fowler's after all. But Mr. Miller was genuinely friendly, if somewhat disorganized, and the money he offered was actually more than she'd make at Fowler's. She suspected he really wanted company more than help.

At noon they shared a pot of soup made on a hot plate in the rear of the store. As they sipped the steaming broth, Mrs. Pine asked if she might tidy up the dusty front window. It hadn't been changed since summer and still displayed an array of beach balls and sand pails.

"Glad to have it taken off my hands," Mr. Miller readily agreed.

After lunch, Mr. Miller produced a small artificial Christmas tree and a string of lights. Mrs. Pine set to work. She removed all the summer items, cleaned the window with a scrubbing brush. She arranged a display of toys to brighten the heart of any child, sprinkled artificial snow over everything, strung the lights along the bottom of the window and ran to a nearby hardware store for tinsel and icicles.

As they stood outside, admiring the window, Mr. Miller agreed that the whole store had a different spirit now. **But some-**

45

thing is still lacking, thought Mrs. Pine. **That little blue wagon in the corner needs dressing up.**

Searching through the shelves and drawers, Mrs. Pine found a beautiful doll. She hadn't seen another like it in the store, and indeed, she thought she had never seen a doll so beautiful. She put it in the little blue wagon, spread the folds of the yellow satin dress and carefully brushed the shiny blond hair.

When Mrs. Pine looked up from her work, the eyes of a small, frail girl met hers through the window. The child was no more than nine or ten. Mrs. Pine smiled and the girl smiled back, pointed to the doll and shook her head in admiration. Then with a sudden embarrassment, the child turned and ran off down the street.

Mrs. Pine noticed the thin, opened coat, the torn stockings, the scuffed brown shoes, one without a heel. From the look of her, mused Mrs. Pine, she'd be lucky to have dinner on Christmas, much less an expensive doll.

But she thought no more of it until the next afternoon when the girl again appeared at the window and gazed longingly at the doll in the little blue wagon. She came again the next day and the next.

By the end of the second week of afternoon visits by the child, Mrs. Pine started hoping no one would buy the doll. She didn't think she could bear seeing the child's disappointment if the doll were gone from the window.

Then one day as the little girl was leaving, Mrs. Pine made up her mind. She approached Mr. Miller and told him she wanted to buy the doll herself.

"I want it for that little girl who comes to look at it every day," she said. "It saddens me to think of that child spending Christmas without that doll."

"You can have it at cost," said Mr.

46

Miller.

On the day before Christmas, Mrs. Pine was busier than usual, but during a lull, she took the doll from the window and wrapped it in some colorful holly paper.

By five o'clock, business had slacked off and the store emptied. Together they watched through the window for the appearance of the child. Mrs. Pine could hardly wait to see the young girl's expression when she would give her the surprise.

Shortly before five-thirty the child came hurrying along the street. But this time she didn't stop and peer in the window. She opened the door and walked straight up to Mrs. Pine.

"Please," she said, "I'd like to buy that little blue wagon in the window. I have enough money now."

Mrs. Pine gave Mr. Miller a startled look.

"The sign in the window says four dollars," the child went on, "and I have enough." From an old wool sock, she poured four dollars and eighty cents in coins onto the counter.

"I—I thought you wanted the doll," Mrs. Pine said softly.

"Oh, it is beautiful," the child replied.

"But I want the wagon for my brother. I came every day to make sure it was still here. He wants a wagon so badly and I don't want him to be disappointed. He's only five." Her eyes were wide with seriousness.

Mrs. Pine fumbled behind the counter to wipe her eyes and blow her nose. She stood up with the package in her hand. "Well, of course you can buy just the wagon," she said. "But if you don't mind, the doll goes with the wagon. You can have both for four dollars."

"That's right," Mr. Miller chimed in. "We hope you both have a very happy Christmas, you and your brother." He glanced at Mrs. Pine. "I know Mrs. Pine and I will."

Mr. Miller brought the wagon from the window and the child left, the wagon trailing behind her and the gift-wrapped doll hugged tightly to her breast. Mrs. Pine stood silently for a moment. Mr. Miller said nothing. It was dark now and a light snow was falling. The colored lights in the window tinted the flakes with soft colors.

"Time to close up," said Mr. Miller. "Merry Christmas, Mrs. Pine."

And indeed it was Mrs. Pine's merriest Christmas ever.

SILENT NIGHT

Silent night, holy night, All is
  calm, all is bright;
Round yon virgin mother and
  child!
Holy Infant so tender and mild,
Sleep in heavenly peace,
Sleep in heavenly peace.

"THEY SAW THE YOUNG CHILD . . ."

◆ ◆ ◆ And when they were
come into the house, they saw the young
child with Mary his mother, and fell down
and worshiped him: and when they had
opened their treasures, they presented
unto him gifts; gold, and frankincense,
and myrrh. And being warned of God in a
dream that they should not return to
Herod, they departed unto their own
country in another way.

MATTHEW 2:11-12

CHRISTMAS EVE IN GERMANY

B. F. "Chuck" Lawley

A fire-red sunset was visible in the west, and a gentle snow was beginning to fall on the prisoner-of-war camp nestled in a clearing surrounded by tall white pines. It was Christmas Eve in Germany, 1944.

The winter had been particularly cold, yet despite our discomfort, hundreds of POWs had trudged through the snow to the crude chapel we had constructed near the middle of the compound.

We'd wanted this night to be a special occasion, so we had topped off our shabby khaki prisoner uniforms with shoestring ties hastily yanked from our winter boots. Now back at the barracks, we tried to maintain a festive spirit, though the quarters were cramped and the winter winds were whistling through chinks in the rudely-constructed walls.

Men who had received Christmas parcels from home began breaking out their delicacies. I had no parcel. The looting of the Red Cross trucks by the Germans had provided someone in Germany with my gifts from home. Curiously, I felt no resentment toward the soldier who had stolen my package; the guards were in many respects as bad off as we were. But as I watched the other guys opening their boxes I felt depressed and left out.

Then Pete, one of my buddies from New Jersey, looked up from rummaging through his parcel.

"Hey, Chuck!" he called to me. "You want some salami and crackers?"

I shook my head and looked away. "Aw, come on," he said, "there's too much here for me!"

He was a bad liar. Tomorrow, when the hunger pains stabbed his gut, he'd be dreaming of that salami. But on this night, Christmas Eve, he wanted to share with me.

Then other men began sharing their gifts with the men who had none. Someone started whistling "Silent Night," and soon we were all singing, hundreds of us, with tears in our eyes, our faces framed by those makeshift ties. I felt Christ's presence then in that terrible place—giving me hope to overcome my despair, showing me love in the midst of fear.

It's been thirty-six years since that Christmas in far-off Germany. Now Christmases with my family and friends are warm, secure and happy times. Yet, each Christmas Eve, as I bend down to tie my shoes in preparation for a festive evening, remember that shoestring tie—and it all comes flooding back to me. Then my spirit is uplifted, I feel truly ready to accept the Christ Child who comes . . . to a cold and lonely stable . . . to a freezing prison barracks . . . to wherever men's hearts are open to receive Him.

THE SCARLET ROBE

Ann B. Benjamin

Aaron was the richest sheep herdsman around Bethlehem. With his fine flock, excellent pastures and loyal shepherds, he was the happiest of men—except for one thing. He and Anna had only one child, their son David, who had been born with a twisted leg.

"He's the best pupil in the synagogue," Rabbi Ben Elim told Aaron and Anna. "But it's too bad—a boy should be able to run and play after his studies are finished."

Aaron thought on these things as he threaded his way through the crowded streets of Bethlehem. These thoughts always made his heart heavy—for though he was a rich man, only a miracle could make him rich in heart.

Aaron was on the street of the clothing peddlers, buying new cloaks for his shepherds, when he spied a scarlet robe among the merchandise of a Persian peddler. This was no ordinary robe—its cloth was of the finest silk and its color was a deep, rich red. It spoke of royalty. **Ah-h, this I must take to David . . .** he thought and quickly paid some gold coins for it.

When Aaron returned from the village, he told Anna and David of the crowds he had seen. "The village inn was full and overflowing," Aaron said excitedly, "and one man had brought his pregnant wife all the way from Nazareth. . . ."

Though he was interested in all his father's excitement about the unusual events of the day, David was curious about the parcel his father was holding. When Aaron handed it to him he could scarcely untie it in his eagerness. The red silk robe glistened in the light.

"The robe is beautiful," little David cried, slipping it over his shoulders. "And

warm too." He ran his fingers on the soft cloth.

"Why, it's fit for a king!" Anna exclaimed, adjusting the coat on David's small body. "And now you look like the son of a king!"

Just then two of Aaron's shepherd boys rushed into the house. "A new, bright star in the sky . . . angels spoke to us." They spoke quickly, one after the other. "A baby was born in the innkeeper's stable last night . . . people flocked to see this extraordinary child." Aaron remembered what the Persian peddler had told him— there was a rumor all through the East that a new King was to be born. Surely **this** wasn't, it couldn't be. . . .

"You **must** come and see for yourselves," the shepherds insisted. Running, carrying the crippled David, Aaron and Anna reached the stable cave which was lighted by a bright star from the heavens. There in the manger was the Baby. They wondered, **could this be the Messiah, the King? The Scriptures did say He would come from Bethlehem.**

David gazed at the tiny infant and at the Baby's parents who seemed so happy though poor. "His mother and father love him, don't they? But they have no clothes

52

for him." He looked at his father. "Do you think he is cold? Maybe . . . Father, may I give him my new robe? You said it was fit for a king."

Aaron looked at his son thoughtfully. "Go ahead, David. Do what you have to do," he said.

Slowly David took off his robe, crawled near the manger and spread his scarlet robe over the sleeping infant. The Baby stirred in His sleep. David turned to crawl back to his parents, then gasped. With a look of wonder and disbelief on his face he slowly stretched out his twisted leg, feeling no pain at all. He managed to get to his feet, stand at his full stature for a moment and then **walked** to his waiting parents.

Later they remembered the prophecy: "He comes to preach good news to the poor, to proclaim release to the captives, the recovering of sight to the blind, to heal the lame, to set at liberty those who are oppressed, and to proclaim the acceptable year of the Lord . . ." They knew that He indeed had come and they had met Him.

SILENT NIGHT

Elizabeth Sherrill

This year on Christmas Eve my husband John and I will get into our car and drive, as always, to our familiar brightly lit church with its swelling organ and banked poinsettia plants. But this year we'll also be driving, in a sense, to another church, a church on the other side of the world, and we'll be thinking of our new Chinese friend, Dr. Li.

Dr. Li is an elderly physician who studied in the United States during the 1930s, but who lives now in Shanghai. John and I met him there early this year on a Sunday when we'd gone to seek out a Christian church we'd heard about. We found the church somewhere in the middle of that enormous city on a street thronged with bicycles and pedestrians all dressed in dark green Mao jackets and loose-fitting trousers. The building was red brick, with tall Gothic windows, and to our surprise it was filled with worshippers; every pew was packed, people sitting in aisles, on the windowsills, standing around the walls.

"How long has this church been here?" we asked Dr. Li.

"A long time," he replied in flawless English, "but only three months ago did it re-open." Then, through the thick spectacles that he wore, we caught a glimmer of tears. "It opened again on Christmas Eve," he said.

For the first few years after the Communist victory in 1949, he told us, churchgoing, though disapproved and discouraged, was still possible. But gradually all churches were closed, boarded up or converted to warehouses—this building in the summer of 1959. For months Dr. Li and his wife tried to accustom themselves to life without the punctuation of that weekly Sunday gathering—especially important where Christians were in such a minority.

Christmas Eve, 1959, was chill and drizzly. At the hospital, it was an evening shift like any other. Only in Dr. Li's thoughts, and perhaps, those of the handful of other Christians on the staff, was there the awareness that this was the night when angels sang.

Dr. Li got back to his two-room apartment around ten, but he could not settle down. At eleven he went into the bedroom intending to get undressed. Instead, he whirled suddenly and headed for the front door. Although not a word had been said, his wife followed him into the deserted street. Through the icy drizzle they walked, moving silently so as to attract no attention.

Left at the corner, across a square, right onto the avenue—both knew without saying it that they were headed for the church. There it loomed ahead, dark and padlocked—but solid too, and somehow comforting. **I really am here,** it seemed to say. **I really came to earth this night, not just as a longing, but in a form you can see and touch.**

As they drew still closer they became aware of other silent walkers. From every side street they came, alone and in twos and threes, converging on the avenue. Soon hundreds were standing shoulder to shoulder in the dark churchyard. Newcomers took up their posts on the sidewalks. For over two hours they stood in the rain while Christmas came. No hymns, no sermon. Only **He is born! He is with us!** in unspoken communion around the shuttered church.

For 20 years, Dr. Li told us, this was their Christmas Eve observance. No outward agreement, so far as he knew, was ever made beforehand to do so. Just, on this night, in homes and apartments all over this part of Shanghai, people silently put on their coats and came to stand here together.

And so it is that this Christmas Eve, when John and I arrive at church we won't have to wait for the communion service to begin. With the first impulse that says "Go!"—with the first longing to share this night with others—the real communion, the undefeatable one, will have begun.

55

GRANDMA'S NIGHT

Fred Bauer

This was my Grandma Strayer's favorite night of the year—one for which she literally prepared a whole year, from one Christmas to another.

When she was growing up, her family was desperately poor and Christmas gifts were few. (At age seven, she once told me, a lone banana in her Christmas stocking was the only present she received.) But in adulthood she apparently was determined to erase the memory of those austere times and so Christmas Eves in her parlor became gala celebrations. Room not taken by an enormous tree, which always seemed to sag under the weight of lights and decorations, was occupied by gaily-wrapped presents, which made it hard to find a seat by the time all her children and their mates and her grandchildren crowded into the room. Buffets and tables were covered with aromatic dishes—cakes and pies, fudges and divinity, popcorn balls, things she'd been preparing for days.

When it came time to begin, she gathered her clan in a tight circle for a reading of the Christmas story from St. Luke. This she followed with prayer, thanking God for the year's many blessings.

Though Grandma had a hard life and worked at all sorts of jobs to supplement the family income (or was it to finance her annual Christmas party?), she could always see more pluses than minuses. Perhaps because of such things as one-banana Christmases.

Finally it was time to open the gifts—grandchildren first—and Grandma always sat on the very edge of her chair, anxious to see whether or not her loved ones were pleased. She usually went to great lengths to choose just the right gift—the extra-long sled, the doll with four changes of clothing, the dress with the special lace—so she watched for reactions with fixed gaze. I can see her now wringing her hands or nervously attending her beautifully-coifed white hair while someone opened one of her gifts. There was never any question that it would be appreciated, but when a child squealed with delight, a sigh would pass from Grandma's lips, and her beautiful round face would glow brighter, I think, than her over-decorated tree. And her eyes, those wonderfully animated blue-gray eyes, they would flash like diamonds behind her rimless glasses. Yes, there was something special about Christmas Eve at Grandma's.

But, alas, she's gone, and so are several others who once made up her happy circle on the night before Christmas. But one thing that remains is my memory of those exciting nights. And whenever I begin to think that all this harried preparation, all the time and money spent on gift giving, is not worth the candle, I think back to Grandma's shining face on her favorite night of the year, and suddenly I remember what Christmas is all about.

THE CHRISTMAS EVE I SMELLED THE HAY

Marjorie Holmes

Christmas Eve and we were late, as usual, herding our family into the hushed candlelit church. The last bell had stopped ringing; every seat was taken. The usher had to lead us up a side aisle to some steps where we could perch behind the choir loft, so close to the manger scene we could smell the hay.

Real hay . . . its pungent scent transporting me back to the sweet smelling hayfields of my childhood. The barns, the mangers. Suddenly I was shaken by a vivid sense of reality. For the first time in my life I realized, "Why, this **really happened!** There actually **was** a girl who had a baby far from home—in a manger, on the hay." A very young girl, probably—because I had recently heard or read that in the culture of Mary's time a girl was betrothed as soon as she went into her womanhood, and married before the year was out.

My own daughter Melanie, thirteen, who had just matured, was sitting beside me. And I thought, astonished, "Why, Mary couldn't have been much older than Melanie—perhaps fourteen—when she bore the Christ Child!"

With this awareness came a thrilling conviction about Joseph. He must have been a young man too; old enough to protect and care for her and the child, but young enough to be deeply in love with Mary. And she with him! Why not? They were betrothed to be married. Surely God, who loved us enough to send his precious Son into the world, would want that child to be raised in a home of love. A place where there was genuine human love between the two who were chosen to be His earthly parents.

I left the church in a state of great excitement. I knew I must write their story. I must make this blessed event as real for other people as it had become for me. That's when I thought of writing **Two From Galilee.** That wonderful Christmas Eve when I smelled the hay.

CHRISTMAS EVE IN THE NURSERY

Sue Monk Kidd

It was Christmas Eve and not a creature was stirring on the pediatric floor of the hospital. I was the nurse scheduled to work. I sat at the desk, staring at a piece of plastic holly on the wall, feeling miserable. I thought about the last-minute shopping I'd wanted to do, the cookies that hadn't been decorated, the caroling, the bowl game on television. It isn't fair, I thought. I'm missing Christmas Eve!

I stood up and dragged my feet down the deserted corridor. I stopped at the sick nursery and sighed. There was that tacky plastic holly again, taped over the door. I pushed open the door and went in. There was only one child in the nursery, a tiny baby a few weeks old. He had a respiratory infection and seemed to be improving. Still, a nursing assistant observed him around the clock. I noticed her standing by his crib as I came in.

"Merry Christmas," she said.

"Some way to spend Christmas Eve," I muttered. I began to scan the temperature chart across the room, when I heard an almost inaudible little gasp.

"My God! He's stopped breathing!" cried the nursing assistant.

I raced for the crib and leaned over the baby. He was limp, turning dusky blue around the mouth. I found a thready heartbeat, but practically no respiration. "Get a doctor and a respiratory therapist," I said. "FAST!"

Seconds ticked. I cleared the baby's throat with suction, pulled back his chin and inserted a tiny plastic airway. Hurry, I kept thinking. I placed the black ambu bag over his nose and mouth and began to squeeze. In and out, in and out, breathing air into his lungs. My other hand held the stethoscope over his chest and listened to his heart patter like a faint little clock winding down.

The nursery door crashed open. In poured two doctors, another nurse, a laboratory technician and a respiratory therapist. We worked frantically in a circle around the crib in a maddening blur of emergency drugs, hissing oxygen and the blip of a heart monitor. Gradually the activity began to slow. Everything that medicine could do had been done. The baby lay unmoving, except for the mechanical rise and fall of his chest by a respirator.

The room grew quiet. Now it seemed

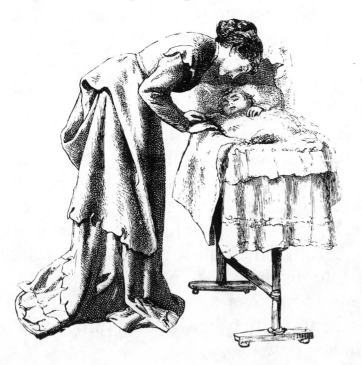

every heart focused on the baby. Nothing seemed to matter except that the limp baby boy breathe again on his own. Lord, help him, I thought.

"Breathe," said a doctor. "Come on, little fellow, breathe!"

"Please God," whispered the nurse beside me.

I saw the same plea in every face as the prayer seemed to move around the crib like a circle of hope.

Suddenly a gurgle drifted up from the crib. Next, a cough . . . and then a tiny cry! The nursery was shattered with silence. The respirator was removed. Everyone waited, all eyes on the baby. He curled his fingers and waved his arms in the air. And then breathed . . . all by himself.

I turned and fumbled with the drug tray, hiding the tears that filled my eyes. I couldn't help but believe that I was standing on the rim of a magnificent miracle. It was Christmas Eve and a baby boy was alive! The extraordinary and precious gift of life had been laid at his feet by Someone other than the little band of people who surrounded his crib. The presence of

Christ seemed to fill the nursery. I knew He had been in the midst of it all. I wondered if perhaps His presence wasn't especially alive in nurseries everywhere, on this night of all nights. And in that moment my heart was drawn to Christ in some deep and holy way I could not explain.

I felt a tug at the back of my uniform, and turned around. "The baby's parents are here," said the ward clerk. "They saw what was going on through the viewing window before I could stop them. They are terribly frightened."

With the baby pink and kicking again, I slipped out and found his mama and daddy in the waiting room. They were holding hands, staring at the cold mist beyond the window.

"Your baby had a difficult time," I said. "But he is much better."

"He's alive?" asked the mother, her hands trembling at her cheeks.

"He's alive and holding his own."

Tears welled up in her eyes. The father's eyes, too, sparkled with the hint of tears. "Thank you," he struggled to say. "Thank you all."

"You've given us a wonderful Christmas present," said the mother. "Our baby's life."

I blinked back tears, unable to speak. I wanted to tell them that it was really **their** son who had given me a gift. He had touched my life with a special holiness. He had helped me find my way back to the Christ-Spirit that dwells deep in the heart of Christmas.

THIS DAY

This Day won't come my way
  again,
So let me take the time,
To make another's holiday
As full of joy as mine.

This Day won't come my way
  again,
So let me freely share,
The blessings of the Season
With those for whom I care.

This Day won't come my way
  again,
So let me spread His love.
As God did when He sent His
  Son,
Christ Jesus from above.

ROSALYN HART FINCH

JOY TO THE WORLD

Joy to the world! The Lord is
  come;
Let earth receive her King;
Let every heart prepare Him
  room
And heav'n and nature sing,
And heav'n and nature sing,
And heav'n and heav'n and nature
  sing.

Joy to the world! The Saviour
  reigns;
Let men their songs employ;
While fields and floods, rocks,
  hills, and plains,
Repeat the sounding joy,
Repeat the sounding joy,
Repeat, repeat the sounding joy.

THE CHRISTMAS ROSE

Velma Seawell Daniels

For my sister Janet and me, like other small children, the days before Christmas dragged on endlessly. As we played together in our small yard across the street from the power plant where our father worked, our hopes for toys and goodies and plans for that wonderful day were the chief topics of conversation. We knew we would be visiting our grandparents in some "distant" city.

There, on Christmas Eve, we would mingle with all the aunts and uncles and cousins. We would sleep on couches, or on one of Grandma's feather beds. Then as soon as the sun came up, we would gather around the tree in the parlor and open our presents. After a morning of us children playing noisily and happily, and the men sitting under the oak trees behind the house talking, and the women working in the kitchen, we would stuff ourselves on chicken and dressing and candied yams and then head for home.

Yes, as Christmas drew near, ever so slowly, those were the thoughts that filled our excited little minds—until we heard it . . .

"BOOM!" A loud explosion.

Janet and I were playing in the front yard close to Father's rose garden. This was his special garden where he spent many weekends on his knees tenderly caring for his rosebushes. Father loved being with his roses more than anyplace else. Now, as the shock wave from the explosion reached us, the very ground shook and the few roses on the bushes quivered and one lone petal fell to the ground.

Noises from the power plant were not unusual. We heard them every day—steam hissing and turbines humming. But this noise was different. It erupted like a clap of thunder—tremendous, deafening, stunning. Then, a huge billowing cloud of smoke arose and rushed skyward to signal disaster. The air was filled with a strange choking odor which I now know was ammonia gas.

Almost at once we heard alarm bells ringing and dozens of voices shouting and screaming. Above the turmoil came the sound of a distant siren demanding the right of way for a speeding ambulance.

Suddenly, Mother was there. With an

arm around each of us, she held us closely as we stared, frightened, at the confusion across the street.

Later, I remember men coming to tell her that our father had been hurt in the accident and that they would take her to him at the hospital. I remember, too, sitting with Janet and a neighbor on our front steps waiting for her to come home.

Finally she came. It was only then, as she stepped from the car, that we broke into tears. She grabbed us up quickly and rushed into the house.

"Girls," she said. "You aren't babies anymore. You mustn't cry. You are old enough to understand what I am going to tell you. Your father was hurt in that explosion. His eyes were burned badly, but I am sure he'll be all right. And there's only one thing he needs—our prayers. So let's start right now."

We bowed our heads and each of us said it: "Please God, make our daddy's eyes all well." Then Mother prayed, "Jesus, we know you can heal him completely. We do not know what to do, dear Lord, so we are going to leave this in Your hands."

Our father stayed in the hospital for a week, but it seemed to be a year. Janet and I were not allowed to visit him, but Mother went every day. Before she would leave, the three of us would sit quietly and hold hands and pray for his recovery. And every day when Mother came home she would tell us about her visit. "His eyes are still bandaged," she would say, "but I am sure he is going to be all right. Our prayers will help make him well."

Then one day she said, "He is worried about his roses and he wants to know if you girls will please water them for him."

So we watered the roses every day and said our prayers for Daddy.

Then Daddy came home with his eyes still wrapped in yards of gauze and great wads of cotton, and the doctor came every day to check his progress and to change the dressings.

Janet and I worried about Christmas. We would not be going to Grandma's house. We'd have Christmas at home, and maybe by that time, our father would be well.

Before the doctor left on Christmas Eve he told my sister and me, "I hope to have a wonderful Christmas present for you tomorrow. I think I'll be able to remove your father's bandages. I can't promise anything, but I'm sure he'll be able to see a little. Maybe only out of one eye, but he'll be seeing something."

That night Janet and I could hardly sleep. "What would he like to see first?" Janet asked, and before I could think, she had the answer.

So, first thing in the morning we dressed in our Sunday clothes and got our special surprise ready. We didn't even think to look for our presents under the tree because we were too excited about our gift for Daddy. As the doctor unwrapped our father's eyes, we both stood by his bed.

"Now, Mr. Seawell," the doctor said, "I want this to be a happy Christmas for you. Open your eyes and take a look."

As our father blinked, and stared into the light for the first time in weeks, there at his bedside we stood. And Janet held up the special gift she had selected—a single, perfectly formed, talisman rose. Tears streamed from his eyes as we ran to kiss him.

"Oh, my darlings," Daddy said as he wrapped his arms around us. "The only things more beautiful than this rose are the shining faces of my two angels. No eyes could behold a greater sight on Christmas morning."

And no children could have received a greater gift. For as we felt our father's strong arms embracing us and saw his eyes bright with happiness, we learned that there is a healing power in the gift of love that transcends all others. And that Christmas we had all felt it . . . and we were never to forget it.

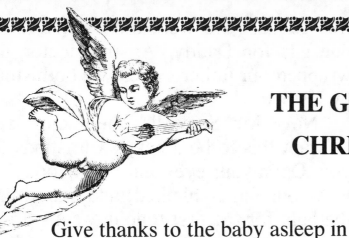
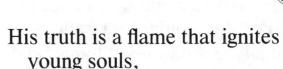

THE GLORY OF
CHRISTMAS

Give thanks to the baby asleep in
the hay,
For it's Jesus who gave us our
first Christmas Day.
A king in disguise, God sent Him
to men,
Revealed to our hearts, He comes
again.

Lord of the galaxies as well as our
earth,
A hymn of the Universe
celebrates His birth.
He gives us His Spirit, His
kingdom's within,
His peace can be ours by
believing in Him.

His truth is a flame that ignites
young souls,
He is comfort to men for whom
the bell tolls,
He restores an image both marred
and grown dim,
He's a constant wonder to those
who love Him.

As we wrap up our presents to
give them away,
We do this because of that First
Christmas Day,
When the Lord of all glory and
beauty and wealth,
Came to earth as a Baby to give
us Himself.

LAVERNE RILEY O'BRIEN

66

PART III
Christmas
Stories and
Poems

THE BLESSING

And when they were departed, behold, the angel of the Lord appeareth to Joseph in a dream, saying, Arise, and take the young child and his mother, and flee into Egypt, and be thou there until I bring thee word: for Herod will seek the young child to destroy him. When he arose, he took the young child and his mother by night, and departed into Egypt: And was there until the death of Herod: that it might be fulfilled which was spoken of the Lord by the prophet saying, Out of Egypt have I called my son.

But when Herod was dead, behold, an angel of the Lord appeareth in a dream to Joseph in Egypt, saying, Arise, and take the young child and his mother, and go into the land of Israel: for they are dead which sought the young child's life. And he arose, and took the young child and his mother, and came into the land of Israel. And he came and dwelt in a city called Nazareth: that it might be fulfilled which was spoken by the prophets, He shall be called a Nazarene.

MATTHEW 2:13-21, 23

69

THE DONKEY

Van Varner

He was not a handsome animal, this donkey. His ears were too long, his body too squat, and his flanks were scarred with the welts of many beatings. He was a common creature, his coat the color of dust, dingy, far from the ivory-white hues reserved, as Scripture said, for the mounts of royalty. Common he was, yet stolid, standing wearily in the cold stable, his muzzle deep in barley, the rich-wet sounds of munching loud in the darkness.

Someone came into the stable. There was a rush of activity. The donkey's ears pricked as he heard the voice of the man, his most recent owner, "Wake up," the man whispered to the lady as a tiny light burst through the darkness. "Bring the Baby. We must go now. Quickly."

The man came to him, and adjusted the rope that served as his halter. This was a good man. The best. No beatings from him. No whips. No kicks. No cries of "Stupid beast!" Over and over again during the three tiring days of travel from Galilee, the man had patted him. "Good fellow," he'd said as the donkey picked his way skillfully among the rocks on the rude trail. The man had been gentle, too, with the lady. She had been heavy with Child, then.

The man led the donkey out into the open air. The sun was just beginning to appear. The lady came out, bearing in her arms a small bundle that she held close and tight. "But where?" she asked the man, fearfully.

"South," said the man. "Egypt, if we can."

The lady drew near the donkey and as the man prepared to help her mount his back, the donkey saw the Child for the first time, and the Child the donkey. In one quick moment the Child reached out and touched the donkey's short, coarse mane. The donkey shivered.

The lady settled on the donkey's back. "Good fellow," said the man as he gave the donkey a pat. And then they were off, the man, the lady, the Child, the donkey.

The morning sun was brightening the earth now, and as its first rays fell upon the retreating figure of the old donkey, they seemed to shimmer. Something had happened to the animal, an extraordinary change. There was pride in the lift of his head; his hooves rose and fell in clean, sharp beats; and his coat—no longer was it the color of dust. Now the donkey's entire body was of a hue befitting a royal Passenger, the color of ivory.

THE BEST SHINE IN PERU

James McDermott

The flight had been one of the roughest Malcolm Eldridge had ever experienced.

At another time he might have enjoyed a trip to Peru. He had visited Lima three years before to help set up a factory plant conveyor system, and now had been grudgingly sent down to repair it. "But it's December twenty-second," he had complained to his supervisor. "I'll miss Christmas completely."

"Our contract with the Peruvians said we'd send a man **immediately** if our system ever broke down, and you're the only man who can get it going again. That's why we pay you so well, remember?"

"Yes, sir." Malcolm Eldridge replied. Once out of the executive's office, he said, under his breath, "And a Merry Christmas to you, too, Scrooge!"

By the time he picked up his suitcase and cleared customs, the airport seemed strangely empty. The throngs had quickly dispersed into a clattering collection of ancient automobiles. He felt a tug at his sleeve and a high-pitched voice said, "Hotel Bol-ee-var?"

"Yes," he said, "Hotel Bolivar. Is there a taxi?"

"Bol-ee-var taxi here ten minutes. While wait I give shine? Best shine in Peru!"

Malcolm looked down at his tiny accoster. He had a mop of jet-black hair and sparkling dark brown eyes, and a look that was half plea, half hope. He had a small shoeshine box in tow.

"Sure."

The taxi was twenty minutes late, but the shoeshine boy was as good as his word. Malcolm's shoes gleamed.

It wasn't until he was in the taxi that he noticed his largest Peruvian bill—worth over $30—was missing. It must have stuck to the bill—worth about sixty cents—that he had handed the shoeshine boy, telling him to keep the change. He had kept the change, all right.

He told the taxi driver to wait and dashed back to the terminal. But the shoeshine boy had vanished. Malcolm Eldridge looked ruefully at his feet. "The best shine in Peru," he said wearily, "worth just over thirty dollars. Welcome to Peru, sucker."

On Christmas Eve one of the plant managers took Malcolm home for a Peruvian-style Christmas. It was very noisy with unruly children squirming everywhere, and the adults drank too much wine and were rather more boisterous than he thought seemly at Christmastime.

The next morning—Christmas Day—Malcolm took a solitary walk to the sea and sat on a high stone wall watching the rollers crest in and smash on the grey rocks below.

"I must be the spirit of Christmas past," he mused to himself. "In my country they care so little about the birth of Christ that it means nothing to send me away from my family at this time. In this God-forsaken land, they drink wine, let the children run wild—it's just another fiesta. Or time to fleece a tourist . . ."

Two days later, his job completed, he was checking in at the airline counter. A porter in a baggy uniform rushed over to him.

"Are you the American from Hotel Bol-ee-var?" the porter asked breathlessly.

Here we go again, Malcolm Eldridge thought. "Yes, I stayed at the Bolivar."

"Did Pepe shine the shoes?" the porter asked.

"Yes, he . . ."

"This from Pepe," the porter said quickly. He held out a gleaming beaten silver belt buckle. In its center the letter "A" had been crudely, but elaborately, engraved. "The father of Pepe dead. The family of Pepe poor. Pepe make Christmas with your money. Shoes for family of Pepe and cooking pot. Pepe say thank you for the money, but . . ." and saying this the porter shrugged.

"What is the letter 'A' for?" Malcolm asked, pointing to the engraving.

"Pepe not know your name. 'A' is for **amigo**—'friend' in Spanish." The porter shrugged again. "Or if not friend Pepe say

'A' is for **Americano**."

"Can you give Pepe a message for me?" Malcolm asked.

"Surely, sir."

"Tell him that he makes me proud to be his friend. Say that because of him I have suddenly had my best Christmas ever— right here in your wonderful country. Tell him, even though he probably won't understand, that he has made me a generous man in spite of myself."

"Oh, yes, sir," the porter said. "Pepe, he understand."

"Yes," Malcolm said, almost to himself, "I guess I'm the one who didn't understand."

O COME, ALL YE FAITHFUL

O come, all ye faithful,
Joyful and triumphant,
O come ye, O come ye to
    Bethlehem;
Come and behold Him,
Born the King of angels.

O come let us adore Him,
O come let us adore Him;
O come let us adore Him
Christ the Lord. Amen.

THE CHRISTMAS TREE SHIP

Glenn Kittler

On stormy November nights, when Lake Michigan roars violently upon its western shores, a legend comes alive. It was on such a night almost seventy years ago that a three-masted schooner with a strange cargo vanished, leaving behind no trace of itself or its crew. The vessel was the Rouse Simmons, but because of its cargo, the children of Chicago called it the Christmas Tree Ship.

Twenty-five years earlier, the Christmas Tree Ship made its first appearance. Sailing magnificently into the Chicago River, it was berthed at the Clark Street Bridge by its proud commander—an 18-year-old boy named Herman Schuenemann.

From all over the city, children came, that holiday season of 1887, to view the unusual cargo: Christmas trees. They were everywhere on the ship, and the vessel looked like an island forest—like a sliver of the vast woodlands in Upper Michigan where the crew had cut the trees to sell in Chicago.

Youngsters loved the glorious sight, and they found, too, that they could always buy their favorite tree for whatever they could afford. No child, even the poorest, went home empty-handed.

Thus, a tradition was born. In the following twenty-five years, the children who had viewed the first Christmas Tree Ship returned with their own children. Herman Schuenemann married and soon had three of his own youngsters who waited each year for the arrival of the Christmas Tree Ship and its wonderland

cargo of evergreens from the north.

In 1912, the vessel began to show its years, and there were many who warned against another journey across the turbulent lake. Herman Schuenemann laughed. "But this is the Christmas Tree Ship," he said. "Nothing could ever sink her. We sail."

On November 21, the schooner, loaded with 50,000 trees, sailed out of Thompson Harbor, Michigan, for Chicago and the children who would be awaiting her. Black clouds of a threatening gale hung over her bow, and by nightfall the lake had burst into a wintry violence.

The Christmas Tree Ship was never seen again; no wreckage ever reached shore, no bodies were ever found.

Many people remembered Herman Schuenemann's conviction that nothing could sink the Christmas Tree Ship. They believed him then, and they believe him still. To them, the ship was a symbol of the Spirit of Christmas, eternal and victorious, and they believe that the vessel still sails the vast mysteries of Lake Michigan.

Should you ask the reasons for their faith, they will take you to the lake shore on a stormy winter night and, in silent confidence, point to hints of the Christmas Tree Ship in the deep, deep evergreen of the wild waves.

A TRADITION ALL HER OWN

Frances E. Wilson

Carefully she placed the small figure of the Christ Child in the crèche. For seventeen years, setting up the crèche just before Christmas had been her special tradition. As she stood back to admire it, she recalled the year it came to her. Yes, came to her with warmth and love.

She was ten years old that first Christmas of the crèche. It was just two weeks before the big day and all the houses on Mulberry Street were decorated with wreaths of green fir and bright red ribbons.

Pamela started counting them as she walked home through the powdery snow that had frosted the town white the night before. She noticed that even old Mrs. Kessel had hung a wreath on her door. It must have taken a lot of effort, Pamela thought, for she was badly crippled with arthritis and could barely get about.

Pamela lifted her feet in high steps and continued marching along. She made a path of big holes as she pushed her feet squarely down into the drifts of fresh snow. She hoped it would snow some more. You need to have snow for Christmas, she thought. Just like you need to have those Christmas customs her teacher had talked about at school that day. Miss Snyder had told the class about the special things people did to celebrate the holidays: putting lights and tinsel on the Christmas tree, wreaths of pine cones, hanging stockings, caroling. Pamela did wish, however, that she had something special she could do at Christmas, a custom all her very own. She thought about that as she walked the rest of the way home.

Once inside the warm house, Pamela hung up her coat and hurried into the kitchen where her mother was chopping nuts and measuring candied fruits for fruitcakes. Pam took a round, red apple from a bowl on the kitchen counter and bit into it. She watcher her mother pour the nuts and fruits into a glass mixing bowl.

"Mother, you always make fruitcakes for Christmas, don't you?" she asked, her elbows propped on the counter top, her eyes studying her mother.

"Yes, I guess you'd say that," her

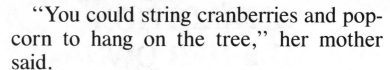

mother answered, stirring the mixture with a wooden spoon. "In fact, fruitcake and floating island pudding are holiday traditions I've known since I was a girl, even younger than you. Some time you could learn to make it, then you'd be carrying on a family tradition."

"I guess so," Pam sighed, tossing her apple core in the trash bin. "What I'd really like though, is a tradition all my own. Dad always picks out the Christmas tree for us and sets it up in the tree stand. Tommy always puts the lights on the tree because he's tall enough to reach all the branches. Why, even Annie gets to place the silver spire on the top of the tree and she's just a baby!" Pam sighed and pushed her brown hair back behind her ears.

Her mother put her arm around Pam's shoulders and gave her a quick hug. "Your daddy used to hold you up to put the silver ornament on top of the tree. Don't you remember that? That's always been the special job for the youngest member of the family."

"That's just it! Everybody in our family has something special to do for Christmas!" Pam bit the corner of her lip. "Everybody but me!"

"You could string cranberries and popcorn to hang on the tree," her mother said.

"That would be O.K. for one time, I guess," Pam said with a shrug. "But I want something more," she narrowed her eyes thoughtfully. "I want something that could really make Christmas special for me, too—every year."

The next day after school Pam walked with slow steps toward home. Her head bent down, she shuffled her feet through the snow. "I just don't feel much like celebrating Christmas this year," she said half aloud. As she reached down to scoop up a handful of snow, she caught sight of a folded newspaper sunk in a pillow of snow at the edge of Mrs. Kessel's yard.

Grabbing the paper, she hurried up the walk and rang the doorbell. She brushed the snow from the paper with her mittens as she waited. She knew it would take Mrs. Kessel a while to answer the door for she walked very slowly using a cane.

"Pamela, my dear," the grey-haired lady greeted her with a smile of welcome. "My newspaper, how nice of you, dear. Won't you come in and visit with me? It's too cold to stand out there." She smiled at Pamela.

78

Entering Mrs. Kessel's living room, Pam stuffed her mittens in her coat pocket and took a seat on the couch near Mrs. Kessel's rocking chair. She did like visiting Mrs. Kessel. She was always so friendly and everyone in the neighborhood liked to listen to her stories. And she was a good listener, too. Pam found she was soon telling Mrs. Kessel all about her wish to have a special Christmas custom, telling her about Mother's special pudding and how Anne was the one who put the top spire on the tree.

"You know, Pam, I believe I have something put away that will interest you," Mrs. Kessel said as she leaned forward in her rocker and pointed toward the dining room. "Go open the right hard door of the buffet and bring me the white, cardboard box you'll find there."

In a minute Pam returned with box tied with white string. "What is it? What's in this box?" she asked. She was finding this an exciting mystery and her fingers trembled as she worked to untie the string.

"You'll soon see, dear," Mrs. Kessel said with a smile.

With a gentle yank, Pam had the cord free. Lifting the box lid, she discovered several packages wrapped in tissue paper.

"Take each of them out, one at a time," Mrs. Kessel instructed. "As you unwrap them you can set them in order here on the rug." She pointed to the space in front of her chair.

Pam had already begun pulling away the tissue. "Oh, what a darling little wooden lamb," she exclaimed as she put the small carved animal on the rug and reached again into the box.

Within a few minutes, she had four more sheep and three long-legged camels lined up on the carpet. She opened a larger package and discovered it contained several shepherds and also three kings. Pam knew they were kings, because they wore crowns on their heads.

"Why, these are the shepherds who took care of all the lambs and the kings who rode on their camels to see the Baby Jesus," Pam cried, her voice was filled with delight. "It's just like the manger

scene in front of our church!"

"That's right, Pamela. It's called a crèche. At Christmas time in my home in Vienna my family always placed these nativity figures and the manger on the mantle about our fireplace."

"This was **your** special custom then, wasn't it?"

Mrs. Kessel nodded. "I haven't set it up for several years now. It is so difficult with my arthritis, you know."

"I'll set it up for you!" said Pamela excitedly. She placed the rustic crib on Mrs. Kessel's mantle and arranged the kings and the shepherds, Mary and Joseph. Carefully she took the tiny figure of the Christ Child and placed it gently in the crib.

"Thank you, my dear," said Mrs. Kessel. "But now I'm afraid you'll have to come back after Christmas and pack them away."

"Oh, I don't mind," said Pamela. "I'll do it very carefully. And next year . . . next year, I'll set them up for you again. I mean—could I, Mrs. Kessel?" Pamela ran to the woman and knelt at her feet, her face bright with anticipation.

"Yes, yes, Pamela, I'll look forward to it," said Mrs. Kessel. "Our little visits mean so much to me."

Suddenly Pamela struck her forehead with the palm of her hand. "This is it," she cried. **"My very own Christmas tradition!"**

For five more years, Pamela set up and took down Mrs. Kessel's crèche at Christmas time, sharing with the elderly woman moments of peace, warmth and friendship. When Mrs. Kessel died, her will stipulated that the crèche should go to Pamela.

Now she stood in her living room, staring at the lovely figures with wonder that filled her every year at this time. As she touched them, her two-year-old toddled in from the playroom.

"What's that, Mommy?"

She picked him up and held him close. "That's Mommy's very own tradition," she said.

He looked puzzled. "Someday you'll understand," she murmured.

THE LITTLEST CAMEL

Shirley Climo

St. Francis of Assisi taught that all the gentle creatures that shared the stable with the Christ Child should share, too, in the anniversary of His birth. So, in many countries, it is a tradition to remember the furred and feathered members of the household at Christmas. In Scandinavia, sheaves of grain are tied atop the roof to feed the hungry birds. In Spain, extra rations are given the cattle in remembrance of the cow who warmed the baby Jesus with its breath. In Belgium, and in parts of France, lambs are brought to the church to be blessed on Christmas Eve.

According to Syrian legend, one animal present at that first Christmas was blessed in a special way. The three Wise Men had traveled many arduous miles upon their camels before they reached the stable.

When, at last, the Magi dismounted to give the Christ Child their gifts, the first two camels also knelt and bowed their heads before Him. But the third camel, young and wearied from so long a journey, stumbled and sprawled beside the manger. The onlookers were horrified, and might have beaten the beast had not the Christ Child stayed them, lifting His small hand. He blessed the little camel and promised that henceforth it should be the bearer of gifts to all children in His name.

That is why children in Syria leave bundles of hay outside their doors on Three Kings Day (January 6). It is their thank you to "the Camel of Jesus," who, they believe, is still faithfully traveling the long miles to bring their Christmas gifts.

CHRISTMAS-LIKE HEARTS

The world at Christmas, is fresh
  and new;
I wish it could linger all year
  through.

Then the shine of Christmas in a
  wondrous way,
Could send its brightness each
  passing day;

And after this season as the New
  Year starts,
We would keep on giving with
  Christmas-like hearts.

JUNE MASTERS BACHER

83

A TREE FOR MIN

DECEMBER

Deborah Grandinetti

I've seen Christmas trees with a variety of trimmings, some adorned with color-coordinated ribbons and velvets; others endeared me with their cookie-cutter and handmade hominess. But none has radiated more warmth than the Cao's scrawny pine with its hand-me-down decorations.

I helped decorate that tree in 1975, the year my parish "adopted" the Cao family. The Caos were six of the several thousand refugees from South Vietnam temporarily housed at Camp Pendleton in California. By mid-October, the family had traversed the country, guided through a maze of charitable agencies to this quiet, Catholic perish on Main Street in Sayreville, New Jersey.

It wasn't until a Saturday evening Mass in early November that I saw them. Three neatly dressed young men, a young woman in a simple, stylish jumper, and a much older woman in native dress followed behind Monsignor Dalton in the entrance procession. A round-faced boy of five or six clung excitedly to Monsignor's hand, letting go reluctantly when the family filed into the pew in front of me.

Mrs. Cao's face alone betrayed the months of anguish. It was ashen colored with deeply-creased wrinkles, visible beneath a thick layer of powder. Her hair, pulled severely back into a soft grey coil, drooped against the starched black mandarin collar of her dress. What a contrast they made, she and the squirming child, who would have climbed into my pew if his older brother hadn't restrained him.

The boy smiled at me and I couldn't help but smile back. His eyes, fringed with thick, dark lashes, were dancing brown orbs of curiosity. It was those eyes I remembered several weeks later when I spoke to Monsignor Dalton about decorating a Christmas tree for the Cao family. I learned then that the boy's name was Min.

As I talked over my idea with the Monsignor, I suddenly found myself scared by the whole idea. I was no longer certain I wanted to do it. How would we understand each other if we couldn't speak the same language? Could I convince my friends to help me?

Monsignor Dalton watched me reconsider, awaiting my answer. I waited for an answer myself. But when our eyes met, his were not the grey tired eyes of an aging pastor, but the dancing black eyes of a child.

"Yes, Monsignor, I still want to do it," I said, and went to tell my friends about it. They greeted the idea enthusiastically.

"My brother-in-law is selling Christmas trees this year," Theresa offered. "I bet we can get one free if I tell him what it's for." Barbara told me she had an extra red metal base and Midge thought her Mom had a separate set of unused ornaments tucked away in the attic. My idea was starting to take on a new excitement.

Then tragedy intervened a week later. Min had been playing near some parked cars outside the apartment complex where he lived when some unsuspecting motorist hit him. He died the next day—a cold, windy Tuesday, two days before Thanksgiving. Monsignor Dalton had tears in his eyes when he asked us to pray for the family. I think we all cried. **How**

could this family bear up under one more loss, especially one as irreplaceable as little Min? I wondered over and over again. I was certain the family would be so burdened with grief that they would decline our offer of a Christmas tree.

"No, Debbie, don't abandon your idea," Monsignor Dalton told me. As he explained it, the Vietnamese customarily make offerings to their dead. So, comforted by our gesture, the Cao family wanted us to decorate the tree in Min's memory. They believed he was looking down upon them and would be comforted, too.

The Tuesday before Christmas my friends Midge, Theresa and Barbara met me as planned. The snow was falling in quiet, nervous flutters as we hoisted the somewhat scrawny-looking pine into the back of the Ford station wagon. Three brown paper bags filled with cellophaned boxes of lights, tinsel, and satiny balls were waiting for us at the rectory back door. Barbara, the last to arrive, tossed the tree base into the back seat and a box of candy canes into my lap as she closed the door.

Mrs. Cao met us at the apartment. As we began to set up the tree, she brought out a photograph of Min and set it on a ledge opposite the Christmas tree. She stood silently looking at the photo of Min. I wanted so much to say something, but the words stuck in my throat. The ache lingered in the air with the scent of pine until the Caos' tabby tangled itself in an open box of garland. We laughed at the cat and at the scrawny, lopsided tree that refused to hold any decorations on one side. Mrs. Cao smiled and then joined us at the tree.

One of the Cao boys began playing a guitar and we gathered around him. Almost effortlessly, his fingers flew through a popular American tune. In broken English, he said he had learned to play the guitar at Camp Pendleton. Soon, voices that had struggled to speak a common language a moment before, were now harmonizing in song.

Staring at the tree, I noticed it didn't look quite so lopsided now. And I began to feel as if I belonged here, in this small circle of newly-made friends. I had been wrong to be so afraid, to think the language barrier would be a problem.

Looking at the photograph on the ledge, I marvelled at the little child who watched us and had drawn us together. And in the same moment, I marvelled at the presence of another Child, who in His wisdom had given us to each other this holy and peaceful Christmas night.

PART IV
Christmas Memories

THE TIE CLIP

Dick Schneider

It was the day after Christmas, 1932, and a blustery wind traced white veins of snow across the sidewalk in front of our house. I glanced out the window of our living room where I was playing with my Christmas toys and the joy of the moment was snuffed as quickly as a candle.

Uncle Emil was coming.

A black sheep in the family, he worked on and off for the Chicago and North Western Railroad. He held the job only because he had lost an arm as a youngster while ducking between some freight cars, and the railroad felt it owed him this much.

However, the loss never seemed to bother Uncle Emil. Often, when his heavy jowls were flushed, he would take a stance like an angry bull elephant in the middle of the living room and boast of how many men he had fought to the ground with his one good arm. Every once in a while he would disappear into the bathroom and reappear ruddier than ever. It took me a few years to realize that it wasn't his kidneys but a pocket flask that prompted these frequent visits.

He had been married once, or twice; no one really knew. And now he lived alone in a room on Chicago's west side.

Uncle Emil talked incessantly of things of no interest to a ten-year-old; of ways to win at the race track, important positions he had turned down at the railroad, and, after several trips to the bathroom, of new speakeasies he had found. Bored almost to sleep, I listened with half an ear only.

One unforgettable year when his voice reached a high intensity, he became quite enthused about a new set of false teeth. Suddenly he took them out and flung them across the room for me to inspect. Trying to hide my disgust, I gingerly handed them back and ate little dinner afterwards.

Thus, every December as the holiday approached, I would complain to my mother about Uncle Emil's impending visit. "But why, Mom, why?"

"Because it is Christmas."

"He **ruins** Christmas."

"He has nowhere else to go," said Mother, her mouth firm, signaling an end to the discussion.

And now Uncle Emil was coming. Two days ago, Mother had given me a dollar to buy a gift for him.

As I entered the five-and-ten, a seed of evil entered my soul. Looking at the worn dollar bill, I could see no reason why I should buy that man a gift when there were so many things I needed. There was a model of the Gee Bee Sportster airplane I had always wanted to build. Its cost seventy-five cents, but I could still find something nice for Uncle Emil with the remaining quarter.

Finding something for twenty-five cents wasn't as simple as I had thought. But the salesgirls were beginning to drape clothes over the counters as closing time neared, and I settled on a cheap gold-colored tie clip.

I eased my conscience with the thought that, after all, he never brought us a Christmas present. At least an aunt brought chocolate coins in gold foil through they tasted of moth balls from a year's storage in her dresser drawer. She always bought her holiday gifts at after-Christmas markdowns.

Uncle Emil settled himself in his usual chair, and again I sat through the usual harangue, interspersed with bathroom breaks.

I had not shown Mother his gift. I wrapped it beforehand and presented it to Uncle Emil in the living room while she added last-minute touches to the dessert.

Just as he unwrapped it, Mother stepped into the living room. One glance at the tie clip and she turned to me, eyes blazing. Then, quickly covering her anger, she said: "Come, Emil, it's time for dinner."

Heaving his ponderous bulk from the cushioned chair, he slipped the tie clip into a coat pocket and lumbered to the table.

After dinner, Mother helped him into his coat and then stood at the living room window watching him walk, head bent into the swirling snow, to catch the street-car.

Retribution rained heavily on me that night. Mother informed me in no uncertain terms that Uncle Emil never wore ties because he couldn't knot them. And, if I had any thought for others, I could see that.

The following spring Uncle Emil died. After the funeral, Mother and I went to clean out his room, a small, dingy chamber that smelled of mouthwash and shaving soap, with a cracked green shade at the window. It was the first time that I saw where he lived.

While Mother packed clothes into a carton for the Salvation Army I studied the walls of his room. Cracked yellowing snapshots were stuck inside the frame of his mirror; here and there an old letter, wrapped in a ribbon. Treasured fragments of those he had loved. And then some-thing caught my eye. I couldn't believe it. Up on the wall, clipped on a Christmas card from our family was the cheap tie clip, tarnished by the past four months.

On the card with it were some words in his labored scrawl. I stood on tiptoes and dimly made them out:

"Christmas, 1932, from my nephew."

Suddenly, Uncle Emil's life fell in on me—his losing battle with the world, his hunger for companionship, his longing to have someone with whom to talk.

The shadowed glint of the tie clip wavered and dimmed in my vision. Wiping my eyes, I moved over to Mother, stumbling gently into her side.

"Mom," I said over a lump swelling in my throat, "I'm awfully glad we had him for Christmas."

She glanced up at the tie clip, and then at me. She reached down and gripped my shoulder for a moment. I think she knew that in Uncle Emil's room I had begun to grow up.

THE WISH TREE

G. S. Carlson

Afew days before Christmas one year, Gayle, my wife, made a decision: We'd all gather around the kitchen table and make Christmas wishes for one another and for ourselves. It would be a sort of thanksgiving, combined with our hopes for the coming year. We'd do it on the day we put up the tree.

"But you've got to be specific," Gayle reminded me and the three kids. "None of this 'hope you have a good year' or 'I'm thankful for my health'—**be specific.**"

Our Christmas tree has since become our "Wish Tree." This is how it works:

1. Each of us writes a note to the other family members, expressing his or her hope for that person in the coming year.

2. Each person writes himself or herself a note expressing a personal wish for the coming year.

3. Finally, each person writes a note about the one thing he or she is most thankful for.

These notes—hand written on different colored pieces of paper and sealed in matching envelopes—are then hung on the tree. Throughout the Christmas season, they remind us that we are a family: each of us is special. At the end of the Christmas season, when the tree comes down, the gaily-colored wish-notes are

put away with the rest of the ornaments and saved until next Christmas. Only at that time do we take out the notes from the previous year, sit down around the kitchen table and read them to see how close we came to realizing our hopes for each other and ourselves.

Some examples:

From Cathie, now 18 and a receptionist-secretary in a Washington, D.C. firm—to herself, in thankfulness: "I am so very thankful that I am stronger and can stand up for myself better." Her parents, meanwhile, have complained for years that she's too strong and stands up for herself all too well.

From David, going on 12—to himself, in thankfulness: "I'm thankful for being baptized." He and I had journeyed to upper Michigan some months previously to visit my family. Daddy, a surprisingly spry 89 now, and a retired minister, baptized Dave while we were there.

And there are the wishes:

Gayle to Cathie: "I wish for you a good car of your own. . . ."

Debbie, who is 16 going on 25, to Cathie: "I wish for you to get your driver's license back." Cathie's license was taken away for a year for medical reasons.

Dad to Cathie: "Lunch with your father more than once in the coming year." We'd never been able to meet downtown for lunch except once the previous year. And so the wishes go . . .

One thing we've discovered is that our wishes for the other are most often things that have concerned that person, too. I think that means that we've been trying to listen to each other.

Whether or not any of our wishes come true (some do, some don't), isn't as important to us as the fact that they are wished—prayed, really. Our Wish Tree becomes a tangible way of showing our love—the most valuable gift a family can give to itself.

GRANDPA'S TALLEST CHRISTMAS

Fred Benton Holmberg

The bicycle was beautiful and brand new. It was under the Christmas tree and had the names of my two sisters, my brother and myself on it. We saw nothing else. I was nine years old and couldn't believe it.

The year was 1940 and for us, like so many other people, the Great Depression was still not over. So the gift was almost beyond our imagination. A friend of Mom and Dad had given it to us and we were thrilled. We climbed on it, over it, danced around it—all four of us trying to ride it through the living room at the same time. Snow hadn't fallen yet that year and all morning long we rode it up and down the street, literally all four of us riding at one time.

By noontime Christmas Day, we were eager for Grandpa to see it. Grandpa and Grandma were coming for Christmas dinner by bus. There had been a time, twelve

years earlier, when there were servants and a chauffeur and two great houses and cars. The Depression took it all; mortgages foreclosed, finally there were ten of us in one small house and no money.

Grandpa was a very proud man. He had been Governor of Massachusetts, President of its Constitutional Convention

and now he was penniless. He was in his late seventies, and very proud, but on this day even his bus fare was borrowed.

"They're coming—they're coming!" my two sisters shouted, seeing two figures getting off the bus.

We were about to rush out with the new bicycle when my brother shouted to me, "Hide the bike, quick." I didn't understand. Then, looking out the window, I saw Grandpa was wheeling a bicycle—worn, bent, beaten, but freshly and badly painted bright red.

Grandpa was smiling. It was the biggest smile I had seen in years. Grandpa walked tall as if displaying a prize-winning racehorse. The four of us looked at each other, and my brother, without saying another word, quickly carried the new bike of the early morning down to the cellar. Then we ran out to greet them.

"Guess who this is for?" Grandpa said, his chest expanding like a proud peacock. "It's not the sturdiest, but . . ."

"We love it, Grandpa!" my brother shouted, rubbing his fingers along the rusted chrome handlebars.

"It's the best Christmas present ever!" my sisters chimed in, lavishing Grandma and Grandpa with hugs and kisses.

We climbed on board and again all four of us tried to get on and ride it. The front tire went flat. We pumped it up. Later we found out Grandpa had gone to the Salvation Army, paid a few pennies for the old bike, taken it home, fixed it as best he could, and then painted it bright red.

We rode only the rickety bicycle the whole time Grandpa and Grandma were there. And Gramps never left the porch that afternoon. He stood there tirelessly watching us race back and forth on the wobbly bike. And I know now that was the best gift we could have ever given Grandpa. For he never looked taller or prouder than when he bent down to get a hankie from Grandma's apron pocket and quietly wiped his eyes.

THE CHRISTMAS CONCERT

Margaret Peale Everett

Three years ago, on December 24th, a special invitation appeared at each of our places at breakfast. It was made of half a piece of construction paper, folded over, with a tiny ribbon poked through holes in one corner. On the front, in bold magic marker, it read:

YOU ARE CORDIALLY INVITED . . .

Our children, Jennifer, age 11, and Chris, age 8, eagerly flipped theirs open and then looked disappointed. As I opened mine, seeing my husband's familiar handwriting, I read:

. . . to a special candlelight concert
of recorded Christmas music
4:30-5:30 p.m.
December 24
R.S.V.P.

"What's this all about?" I asked Paul. "You'll see."

"But I don't have time to sit for an hour listening to music tonight. We have to eat an early dinner, be at church at 7:30, and I still have presents to wrap and . . ."

"You don't have to come," he interrupted. "Just R.S.V.P. 'no.' I will be there and I'd love to have any of you who want to, join me."

The children said 'no' immediately, but I said nothing, deciding to leave it on the back burner of my mind during the day.

At 4:30, frankly, I'd forgotten the invitation. I had just dashed in from a last-minute errand, discovered puddles of melted snow on my newly-cleaned kitchen floor and was about to track down the culprit, when I noticed that Paul was lighting all the candles on the first floor of our house.

"What are you doing?"

"It's time for the concert."

Paul flipped on the stereo and the music began. The beautiful sounds of Christmas filled our home. One song after another—from the **Messiah** to **Joy to the World,** from choir to solo to instrumental—engulfed me, and I finally stopped my activity and joined Paul in the living room. There, together, as dusk turned to night, we watched the flickering candles send shadows of dancing light all over the room, our bodies and souls quieted by the music proclaiming Christ's birth.

We have now received three such invitations. This past Christmas our daughter, now 14, listened from the family room, our son from the kitchen. Each of these rooms was lit only by candlelight. This year my parents visited us. As they opened their invitations, I could "read"

their thoughts: **"I can't sit for an hour listening to music."** However, when 4:30 arrived, they joined us—just to be polite, I'm sure! For one hour we sat still and let the timeless music of Christmas infuse our thoughts and quiet our hearts. And as they left us for the airport, two days later, my father said, "I'll never forget that wonderful hour of music. I really felt the spirit of God preparing me to celebrate Christmas."

These days we talk a lot about remembering the spirit of Christmas, but for me, at least, it is still too easy to get all caught up in things to do and places to go. Now I have at least one hour—on December 24th—which brings me back to the heart of Christmas and gives us a chance to meditate on the importance of Christ's birth to us.

THE LAST CHRISTMAS TREE

Charlie Wittman

My Grandma, who lived with us after Grandpa died, was a remarkable, often feisty lady who loved the Christmas season more than any other time of the year. Her blue eyes sparkled as she hobbled on her single crutch from one store to another, with me at her side, shopping for our Christmas tree—a job that was hers, and hers alone.

One bitter-cold Christmas Eve—I was a little more than twelve, and Grandma was still on her crutch, frail and bent and with very poor eyesight—we stood at our favorite sidewalk tree store surrounded by pines of all sizes and shapes.

Stomping my feet in a futile effort to ward off the bone-chilling air, I impatiently waited for Grandma to pick **her** tree. "C'mon, Grandma, here's a nice one."

But I got that familiar, "No, that's just not right."

I knew she was wrong. What I had led her to was a full and healthy tree, lush and rich in branches—the kind of tree Grandma had selected for so many Christmases gone by.

But Grandma gravitated toward what to me was a puny, underourished stick of a pine. "This one," she demanded. "Grandma, that's terrible!" I said contradicting her, "Look, its branches are so skinny."

"This one's just right. Just right," she repeated firmly. She could tell I was disappointed.

"Wait 'till you see how pretty it'll be. You'll see," she said, trying to heal my wounded spirit.

Soon after we arrived home, Grandma complained about being tired. Mom and Dad urged her to lie on the couch and rest while we decorated the tree. How we were going to make this one pretty, I honestly didn't know. I just knew Christmas couldn't be the same with this little stick-of-a-tree in our living room.

But Dad strung the colored blinking lights perfectly. Mom used all her home-made decorations—hand-painted wooden animals and tiny checked-gingham doll figures—and hurriedly made more from popcorn and balls of thick red and green yarn. Grandma wakened to see the finished tree and beamed her approval. She sat up on the couch and took in the tree's full majesty.

"You see," she whispered, and motioned me to sit next to her, "this tree is just right, Charlie. It's one of God's creations, too. No matter how deprived and unwanted it may appear to be, look what love and care can do."

I looked up at her deep, misty eyes and I knew she was right. Never had I seen her more radiant. I was certain I could see reflections from the tree lights actually dancing atop her head of abundant white hair!

Mom and Dad lowered the house lights, then joined us on the couch. For a few quiet moments we sat together, captivated by the warmth of the stick-of-a-tree transformed into a brightly glowing Christmas symbol. Even then I somehow knew this Christmas would always be special. And it was. It was Grandma's last

Christmas, her last Christmas tree, her last lesson to me:

"Look what love and care can do for the deprived and unwanted."

I pray I never forget that.

THE CHRISTMAS DOLL

Pat Sullivan

The doll had been beautiful once, with golden curls, big blue eyes that opened and closed, and a rosebud of a mouth. But now she was old, and her clothes were torn and ragged. The curl was gone from her hair, and it was patchy, and bald in spots. Her eyes wouldn't open, and the sawdust was coming out of a torn spot on her leg.

Mamma told me that if I was good, Santa would bring me a new doll for Christmas, so, relieved, I said good-bye to Annabelle and tossed her out on the trash pile behind our house.

It was December, 1934. That was a very bad year for most families. No jobs, no money. "It will be a skimpy Christmas for the children of the neighborhood this year," I heard Mamma tell her friend. "They will be lucky to have shoes on their feet, and mittens for their hands."

I didn't worry much about such things. The only thing on my mind was a new baby doll, like the one I had seen in a downtown store.

My best friend was Rosa who lived next door, in the basement apartment. Rosa's Mamma was sick in bed most of the time. I heard the grown-ups say she needed a lot of rest and quiet. Rosa took care of her younger brothers and handled the job of being "the little mother" without complaint.

Christmas Day finally came, and I could hardly wait to open the boxes under the tree with my name on the tags. The five of us children got shoes, and mittens, and a new winter coat. But best of all, we each got a new toy. I must have been very good, because my box held a sweet little baby doll, dressed in yellow organdy, with a tiny baby bottle, and a whole layette of clothes.

I ran next door to show Rosa my new doll. Rosa's Mamma was sitting up in a chair in the parlour. She even had her hair combed and a pretty dress on. Rosa saw me and beamed. "I got a doll for Christmas, too," she said. Sitting under the little tree was **my old doll, Annabelle.** Only now, she was more beautiful than ever. She had new curls, her eyes were fixed, and someone had made her a fluffy pink dress and bonnet.

I opened my mouth to say something, but no words would come out. Rosa stared at me sternly and silently and I knew I had better not say anything and spoil her Mamma's Christmas.

Rosa ran to her mother and took her little thin hand and kissed it. "I love her already, Mamma," Rosa said, hugging old Annabelle close to her heart. Her mother smiled a wide smile—the first time I had seen her so joyful. Her cheeks glowed with color and her eyes sparkled with brightness. Then Rosa went to her father, who was cooking the Christmas dinner, and gave him a hug.

"I love you, Daddy," said Rosa softly. "She's the most beautiful doll in the whole wide world!"

Rosa's father smiled happily, and sang as he stirred the spaghetti. And I'll always remember their Christmas, plain and unadorned, but filled with the richness and tenderness of loving parents and a child who knew that the gift of **receiving** can be the most generous gift of all.

OUR "OUT-OF-THE-BLUE" CHRISTMAS

Doris C. Crandall

It was Christmas Eve, 1933. Mama was preparing to bake her "hard-times fruit cake." So called because the only similarity to fruit it contained was prunes, but it was, to our family, an extra-special cake. My sisters, Lottie, Vivian, Estelle and Dolly, and I sat around our kitchen table shelling pecans for the cake.

None of us, except Mama, was enthusiastic, and I suspected her gaiety was partly put on. "Mama," I asked, "why can't Grandma and Aunt Ella, and Aunt Fran and Uncle Hugh, and all the cousins come for Christmas like last year? We won't even have any music unless Joe comes and brings his guitar."

We wouldn't miss not having a Christmas tree because we'd never had one, and Mama and Daddy had prepared us for the possibility of no presents, but the thought of no visitors or music really subdued our spirits. Dolly, aged five and the youngest, sobbed.

"Why'd we have to move, anyway?" she asked, sniffing. So Mama again explained her version of dust-bowl economics.

"When we had to give up our farm we were lucky to find this place to rent, even if it is too far for the relatives to come. Don't worry, though," Mama reassured us, "Why, God might send us company for Christmas right out of the blue if we believe strong enough." She began to mash and remove the pits from the boiled prunes.

As we worked, a wind came up and whistled through the newspaper we'd stuffed into the cracks in the corners. A cold gust blasted us as Daddy entered through the back door after doing the chores at the barn. "It looks like we're in for a blue norther," he said, rubbing his hands together.

Later, Daddy built up a roaring cow chip and mesquite fire in the pot-bellied stove in the living room, and we were about to get into our flannel nightgowns when someone knocked on the door. A traveler, wrapped in his bedroll, had missed the main road and stopped to ask for shelter from the storm for the night.

"Mind you," he said, when he'd warmed himself and had a cup of hot coffee, "I don't take charity. I work for my keep. I'm headed for California. Heard there's work to be had there."

Then Mama fixed our visitor a cozy pallet behind the stove. We girls went into our bedroom and all crawled into the same bed for warmth. "Reckon he's the one Mama said God might send out of the blue for Jesus' birthday?" I whispered. Dolly yawned.

"I'm too young to know," she said.

"He must be. Who else'd be out in weather like this?" Lottie said, and Vivian and Estelle agreed. We snuggled, pondered, and slept.

At breakfast our guest sopped biscuits

and gravy. "I never had a family that I remember," he said, "can't recollect any name 'cept Gibson. You can call me Mr. Gibson if you want." He smiled, revealing gums without teeth. Seemingly, he had no possessions beyond his bedroll and the clothes he wore, but he pulled a large harmonica from his pants pocket and said, "I've always had this. Want me to play something?"

So Mr. Gibson spent Christmas Day with us, and what a delight he was. He helped with the work, told us stories, and played all the beloved Christmas songs on his harmonica. He played by ear as we sang church hymns. After much pleading on our part, he agreed to stay one more night.

The next morning, when we awakened, Mr. Gibson was gone. I found his harmonica on the kitchen table. "Oh, Mama," I cried, "Mr. Gibson forgot his harmonica—the only thing he had." Mama looked thoughtful.

"No," she said softly. She picked it up and ran her palm over the curly-cues etched in the metal sides. "I think he left it on purpose."

"Oh, I see," I said, "sort of a Christmas present. And we didn't give him anything."

"Yes, we did, honey. We gave him a family for Christmas," she said, and smiled.

We never saw Mr. Gibson again. Daddy had an ear for music and quickly learned to play the harmonica. Through the years it brought many a joyful memory of that unforgettable Christmas—the Christmas when God sent us Mr. Gibson right out of the blue—a blue norther, that is—because He knew how much a man with music, who longed for a family, and a family without music, who longed for company, needed each other.

CHRISSY'S SHELL TREE

Velma Seawell Daniels

Christmas was only a week away that day I visited what I call "the shell tree."

I had driven down to our summer cottage at the beach to pick up a couple of books I needed for an article I was working on.

So, on this sunny December day, I slipped off my shoes and set out for a walk down the beach. "How good to be alive—and here," I said to myself, as the wind's playful fingers ruffled up my hair, and its salty perfume reminded me that it was clean and unpolluted.

Even my feet felt happy as they headed for the shell tree. It was at the lower end of the island, about a mile away, and I was curious to know if it was still there.

I had learned the true story of the shell tree from Chrissy Woolley, a dear friend and neighbor who told about it on her Christmas card one year.

"One day, after gathering shells for a collection for each of my children at school," she wrote, "I started for a long walk to the point of the island. Suddenly I was struck with the thought of gathering broken shells. Everyone gathers beautiful shells, but why not gather broken ones? I started picking up only the shells which were broken or had a hole in them. By the time I reached the point of the island, I had quite a collection. I noticed a bare weather-beaten tree at the edge of the

mangrove, and the thought of decorating it with the broken shells came into my mind."

"What joy!" she continued. "While putting the shells on the tree, God showed me the message He was giving me. God has a place for broken things! He is the One who can ease our brokenness, heartache, defeat and discouragement and mold us to what He would have us to be."

As I walked on the beach, I thought about Chrissy's tree and what it meant. "I should look for a shell of some kind to add to it," I thought. So, I started searching for something suitable—obviously something broken. Several times I picked up one, only to discard it a few minutes later for one I liked better.

Then, when I was almost within sight of the tree, I saw what I was looking for. "It's just exactly what this old tree needs," I said aloud.

The tree was just as I remembered it. Some of the more recent additions were

bright and colorful. Others had been bleached white by several years in the sun. Right at the top, a small dried up twig stuck out as though waiting for my gift to be added.

Stepping on the lowest branch of the tree, I placed my offering into the twig.

I stepped back to look at my handiwork. A starfish—whole, not broken—crowned the tree.

"There you are," I said. "Today, instead of being just an old tree holding broken shells, you are a true Christmas tree standing on the beach to honor the Baby Jesus on His birthday. And this time one item is whole—The Star—because God is whole. Like the Star of Bethlehem, He is always looking down on the helpless and broken."

THE TRUTH OF A TOY

Richard Schneider

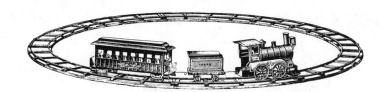

One usually does not remember **all** that happened when one was seven years old, but after fifty-one years I can still recall a particular Christmas moment in vivid detail. And I think now that what I experienced became my first step to adulthood. Let me explain . . .

We had celebrated in Old-Country fashion with the opening of gifts on Christmas Eve. After each of us brothers dutifully recited a memorized Bible verse and sang a carol, we were allowed to open the gifts Kris Kringle had placed under the tree.

It was a large rectangular box. It looked as if it might contain what I had dreamed about for months but had not even dared to ask for . . . Yes, Kris Kringle **knew.** There it lay. A wind-up **American Flyer** train.

Stunned, I reverently lifted the engine, tender and two red-enameled passenger coaches out of their box. Emblazoned on my memory is the little locomotive. Resplendent with red driving wheels, its shiny black boiler was encircled by a brass band which glistened in the shimmering tree lights. As I sat staring at it, I was transfixed with a pleasure that seemed eternal.

Then I heard it—though no one else seemed to. Something or someone whispered: **This will not last. You will grow older. Things like this will not always be a part of your life.** A sadness engulfed me, and my joy waned as I became aware of my growing self.

The moment passed; I wound the little train and sped it merrily on its shining circle. But my pleasure in it was altered.

I think now that in that moment I began to sense that my life on earth is but a shadow; that all things are transitory. I was beginning to be prepared for the message of the One Whose birth we celebrated: "I am the resurrection and the life. Whoever believes in Me will live, even though he dies; and whoever lives and believes in Me will never die."

Now when I feel myself becoming engulfed by concerns, fears and, yes, even joys of a moment, I can close my eyes and still see that gleaming **American Flyer,** clicking 'round and 'round its track. And I remember. **This will not last. Eternity is in Him.**

THE DOLLHOUSE

Eleanor V. Sass

It happened to me the year I turned six. It was an extra-special Christmas, but it was a long time later before I understood why that was so.

As was the custom at our house, Christmas Eve afternoon I had helped my father trim the tall balsam that stood in the place of honor in the corner of our living room. Daddy always made a point of explaining why we decorated our tree in advance of St. Nick's anticipated visit.

"Santa is very busy making toys; he has so many last-minute jobs to finish, he appreciates it when we help him this way." I never questioned my father's words. Anything to help Santa Claus was fine with me.

After the tree-trimming and an early supper, I would be hustled off to my room. Years later, when I no longer "believed," my mother told me that it was the only night in the year when she could get me to bed without a protest. After tucking me in, Mother would turn off the lamp, raise the window shade and peer out into the darkness. "Oh, I see Santa's sleigh and reindeer on Marguerite's roof," she'd exclaim. "Better go to sleep right away, Eleanor. You wouldn't want him to find you awake." Marguerite was my best friend. We played together every day. We also fought and made up constantly. I figured that if Marguerite was judged good enough to rate a visit from Santa Claus, then, surely, my house would be the next stop on his list, so I'd close my eyes and will myself into the land of Nod.

Hours later (though it seemed like only minutes), I'd awaken to the sound of sleigh bells receding and Daddy's voice calling out, "Goodbye Santa! See you next year!" Then I'd hear the front door slam and know—without a doubt—that Santa had been to our house! Mother would appear in the doorway to urge me into my bathrobe, though I needed little urging. Charged with electric excitement, I'd scoot to our living room, where Mother, Daddy and I would open gifts.

But on this particular Christmas Eve, the living room was packed full of people. Rubbing my eyes, I began to recognize faces: My grandparents sat on the couch. Uncles and aunts were everywhere; sitting, standing, kneeling on the floor. I looked from one face to another . . . Aunt Billie, Uncle Charlie . . . They were all there and everyone was beaming. **Why were they here?**

Suddenly my dazzled eyes saw what they were waiting for me to see: a dollhouse. It stood about four feet high on a movable platform. Painted yellow with a dark green roof and front door, I could see white curtains behind every window. Daddy unhooked the front and back of the house so I could peer inside, and what I saw caused my little-girl's heart to leap. A wooden staircase with a bannister went from the first-floor entrance hall all the way up to the third-floor playroom. Every room was wallpapered and carpeted. In the living room, a tiny crystal Christmas tree graced a baby grand piano that stood next to a chintz-covered couch. The second-floor guest room, all done in blue and white, had a bed with a blue lace coverlet. Flanking it were two circular end tables. The feature of the nursery was a baby's bassinet of pale yellow netting. Lively clowns danced across the wall behind it. Little pictures hung everywhere; small tables held tiny lamps or glass ornaments. There was even a broom closet that opened to show a mop, pail and dustpan. It was a seven-room dream house, and I was convinced that Santa had given me the most wonderful gift in the whole world; and all those people who filled our living room had come to see it . . .

It was several years before I learned that every part of my dollhouse had a living creator. Beginning with blueprints, my father and uncles had sawed wood, hammered nails, painted the exterior. Twenty-four pairs of white curtains had been lovingly sewn by Grandmother Parry. Aunt Billie, who worked for an interior decorator, had collected wallpaper and carpet remnants. The chintz couch was the handiwork of my mother.

The yellow bassinet in the nursery came from the talented needle of Aunt Emma. And if you looked closely, you could see that those guest-room end tables were empty cotton thread spools, painted blue and white.

On that Christmas Eve I thought the gift was mine alone. But today, forty years later, when I think about that dollhouse, the planning, the cooperation and the unselfish effort that went into it; how each person gave his or her special talent to create a single gift that symbolized family togetherness, I know that the magic of that night belonged to all of us.

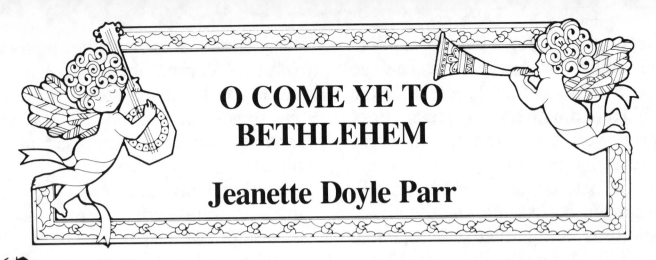

O COME YE TO BETHLEHEM

Jeanette Doyle Parr

Old Ebenezer Scrooge, during his pre-dream days, would have been proud of me that Christmas season. I'd started sprinkling "bah, humbugs" around just two short weeks after Thanksgiving.

Weakened by a recent bout of flu, I was physically and mentally exhausted. For the first time in my life, the Christmas season wasn't proving to be a time of spiritual uplift.

Oh, I'd seen the looks my children had exchanged each time I snapped about Christmas-cookie messes, or tried to hurry clumsy little hands as they wrapped presents. My husband began retreating each time I lamented the high cost of gifts and how commercial Christmas had become, and it wasn't long until even the

And each morning, determined that **this** day would be better, I'd vow to be more patient. But by late evening, I was usually complaining about, or to, someone.

Now, on December 22nd, I had another problem. Try as I might, I couldn't get the angel wings straightened on my little girl's costume.

"Put it on again, Kris. Let Mama see what she needs to do."

Happily Kris put on her costume and slipped her halo over her shining blonde hair. The left wing tilted toward the floor.

"Can I practice my song while you fix me, Mama?"

"I suppose so," I sighed, "just don't wiggle."

Her back to me, she began singing in her thin, childish voice.

Joy, Phil and their trumpet,
Oh come ye, oh come ye to Bethlehem. . . ."

My hands stilled. Unexpected tears spilled from my eyes, ran down my face, and splashed on the glittering wings.

Oh come all ye hateful . . . that was me all right. No wonder Christmas hadn't been the same. I hadn't gone to Bethlehem.

Not once during the entire holiday season had I paused to reflect on the miracle in the manger. My early-morning quiet times, usually devoted to scripture reading and prayer, had been filled with extra baking, wrapping and sewing.

Kris wiggled around to face me. "Are you crying because I sang too bootiful?"

"Yes, baby, because it was so beautiful, just like you . . . and like Christmas." I gave her a big hug and silently vowed that the rest of Christmas **would** be beautiful, because I would take my hateful spirit to Bethlehem. I smiled again. Joy, Phil and their trumpet—we'd all go to receive the eternal gift.

THE CHRISTMAS NO GIFTS CAME

Drue Duke

I'll never forget the first Christmas I spent away from my parents and my sisters, the Christmas I thought I'd receive no gifts.

I was a war bride, living in El Paso, Texas, where my soldier husband was stationed. Because we were saving for a trip to California the next month, we agreed we would not exchange Christmas gifts.

We bought a tiny artificial tree and put it on a table, ready to receive the gifts we knew would come from our families in Georgia and Connecticut. Each time the mail truck stopped at the apartment house I expected the buzzer to our first-floor apartment to sound. But this did not happen.

Christmas Eve came, and around seven o'clock that night Bob was at the hall telephone, calling the post office. As soon as he walked into our apartment, I knew from his face what he had learned. There would be no more deliveries tonight. There would be no gifts to open on Christmas morning.

"I'm sorry, honey," he said. "I'm sure our folks just didn't realize how long it would take for packages to get all the way across the country."

I looked at our pitiful little tree and thought of the floor-to-ceiling tree I knew would be in the music room back home.

"It's not fair!" I cried. "We're way out here, all alone, and we've got no Christmas!"

Just then our door buzzer sounded. Bob opened the door, and a young man dressed in a khaki uniform like Bob's stood there.

"Merry Christmas!" he said. "I think we must be the only ones left in the building. I saw you in the hall, using the phone." He stuck out his hand. "I'm Ned Rogers from the third floor. My wife and I wondered if you'd come up for some fruitcake and coffee and go to the midnight service with us?"

Bob accepted readily and I was not opposed to going. After all, what else was there to do?

It was a pleasant enough evening. The four of us exchanged background information about ourselves. They could not go home to Ohio because Ned, like Bob, could not get a furlough over Christmas. They sympathized with us over our lack of gifts, and I moved my chair to keep from seeing their pile of gaily wrapped packages. I was actually seething with anger at our families, at the post office, at everything and everybody and, worse, was jealous of these people who were trying to be our friends.

I was just about as poor a candidate for church attendance that night as anyone could be. But I climbed with the others into the bus that took us to the downtown Methodist church.

The church was crowded and we had to sit at one side near the back. There was no light except from candles burning in the altar area and in each of the windows along the side walls. The organ played softly and there was a gentle hum of voices as friends wished each other a

Merry Christmas.

Abruptly the music stopped. A hush fell over the crowd. And then from the nearby town clock came the first vibrating **bong-g-g** of midnight.

Instantly light flooded the church as though a million watts of electricity had been fed in. The heavy vestibule doors were flung open and the glorious announcement, "Joy to the world, the Lord is come!" rang out from a white-robed choir moving down both aisles toward the altar. The congregation swept to its feet and raised its voice to join the choir. Above it all, I could hear the clock still proclaiming the birth of a new day, Christmas Day.

My tight, angry, bitter, jealous heart soared within me until my body could not contain it. It burst into a thousand fragments of remorse and repentance for itself and left in its place a glowing flood of love and gratitude.

"The Lord is come! Let earth receive her King!"

My voice rang out with the others. My eyes sought Bob's face and found him smiling. His hand reached out to find mine. And, as with fingers laced together, we sang lustily, we both knew the truth—we were not without gifts. The material things that come wrapped in fancy paper are only symbolic of the **real** Gift of Christmas, the One wrapped in love and swaddling clothes—The Christ Child, Son of the Living God.

TO HAVE CHRISTMAS

Dina Donohue

In the locket of my memory is a picture of a forlorn little boy I saw in an orphanage some twenty years ago. I never even knew his name. Yet, in a way, he has haunted me ever since, especially at Christmas.

I had made the two-hour trip to the orphanage to help my young daughter's Brownie Scout troop. The girls had worked to earn money to give a Christmas party at the cottage housing the four-to-six-year-old boys.

There must have been about twenty-five of them waiting for us in a large, almost bare day room. As soon as they saw the Brownie scouts and leaders in their uniforms, most of the children rushed forward and surrounded us. The more daring started to pat the sleeves of the women while others hung back on the outside of the circle. One little boy just kept stroking my sleeve without saying a word.

"Take me home with you," one child called out. Others took up the chant. The attendants in charge herded them back to a row of wooden seats lined up against the wall. The seats had a hinged lid which lifted up, giving each child a private chest for his belongings.

"Santa Claus is very busy, so he asked the Brownies to help him give you a party," one of the leaders announced. Then she, the other grownups and the Brownies distributed gaily-wrapped packages to each boy, and helped them open their gifts.

I checked to make sure that every child had a toy, and noticed one boy who had none. He was sitting quietly on his seat: a scrawny child with straight brown hair falling over his forehead, almost covering large blue eyes.

I went over to him and handed him one of the extra gifts. "Here, dear," I told him. "This is for you, for Christmas."

"I have one." His voice was very low.

"Well, don't you like it?" I asked.

"I didn't open it." He was silent for a moment. Then he jumped up and lifted the lid of his seat. I could see a wrapped package inside.

"I'm saving it," he explained. "My daddy is going to find a mommie for me and then we'll have Christmas."

I felt my eyes mist. I hugged him close and his taut little body relaxed against me. For a moment I was his mother. Then, suddenly shy, he pulled away. I thrust my package into his hand.

"This is to play with now. Save your other present for later."

I stayed with him while he unwrapped a yellow dump truck and started to push it back and forth. Afterwards, I was busy handing out ice cream and cookies and playing games with the children. Then we had to leave for our long ride home. The attendants again herded the orphans back to their seats. My eyes searched for the shy youngster. He saw me and gave a wistful, tentative smile. Then, with his fingers almost curled, he moved them slightly as if he were a baby waving "bye-bye." There was no time for me to do anything but smile and wave back.

Now, years later, I'm still haunted by the boy. I wonder if his father ever found a mother for him so that he could "have Christmas."

To have Christmas with loved ones: Is there a greater gift?

118

MY CHRISTMAS DISCOVERY

Norman Vincent Peale

Some of my most impressionable boyhood years were spent in Cincinnati. I still remember the huge Christmas tree in Fountain Square—the gleaming decorations, the streets ringing with the sound of carols. Up on East Liberty Street, where we lived, my mother always had a Christmas tree with real candles on it, magical candles which, combined with the fir tree, gave off a foresty aroma, unique and unforgettable.

One Christmas Eve when I was 12, I was out with my minister father doing some late Christmas shopping. He had me loaded down with packages and I was tired and cross. I was thinking how good it would be to get home when a beggar—a bleary-eyed, unshaven, dirty old man— came up to me, touched my arm with a hand like a claw and asked for money. He was so repulsive that instinctively I recoiled.

Softly my father said, "Norman, it's Christmas Eve. You shouldn't treat a man that way."

I was unrepentant. "Dad," I said, "he's nothing but a bum."

My father stopped. "Maybe he hasn't made much of himself, but he's still a child of God." He then handed me a dollar—a lot of money for those days and for a preacher's income. "I want you to take this and give it to that man," he said. "Speak to him respectfully. Tell him you are giving it to him in Christ's name."

"Oh, Dad" I protested, "I can't do anything like that."

smile came to his face, a smile so full of life and beauty that I forgot that he was dirty and unshaven. I forgot that he was ragged and old. With a gesture that was almost courtly, he took off his hat. Graciously he said, "And I thank you, young sir, in the name of Christ."

All my irritation, all my annoyance faded away. The street, the houses, everything around me suddenly seemed beautiful because I had been part of a miracle that I have seen many times since—the transformation that comes over people when you think of them as children of God, when you offer them love in the name of a Baby born two thousand years ago in a stable in Bethlehem, a Person Who still lives and walks with us and makes His presence known.

That was my Christmas discovery that year—the gold of human dignity that lies hidden in every living soul, waiting to shine through if only we'll give it a chance.

My father's voice was firm. "Go and do as I tell you."

So, reluctant and resisting, I ran after the old man and said, "Excuse me, sir. I give you this money in the name of Christ."

He stared at the dollar bill, then looked at me in utter amazement. A wonderful

THANK YOU, GOD

We're coming to that time of year
That's filled with joy and love and
   cheer.
The gifts are wrapped, the
   wreaths are hung,
The trees are lit, the carols sung.
But midst our hurried rushed
   December,
Let's stop—let's remember:
That through a Baby's lowly
   birth,
God gave His greatest Gift to
   earth.
And we who in His name believe,
The gift of LIFE we have
   received.
With all the tasks we've got to do,
Let's take the time to say, "Thank
   You."

Donna Russell

CREDITS: "Our Jesse Tree," by Mildred Tengbom, "Christmas Card Friends," by Laura Norman, "Santa Lucia," by Ann Lindholm, "My Merry Month of Christmas," by Nita Schuh, "Christmas Eve in Germany," by B. F. "Chuck" Lawley, "Grandma's Night," by Fred Bauer, "Christmas Eve in the Nursery," by Sue Monk Kidd, "The Christmas Tree Ship," by Glenn Kittler, "The Wish Tree," by G. S. Carlson, "The Dollhouse," by Eleanor V. Sass, "Grandpa's Tallest Christmas," by Fred Benton Holmberg, "The Christmas Concert," by Margaret Peale Everett, "The Last Christmas Tree," by Charlie Wittman, "Our 'Out-of-the-Blue' Christmas," by Doris C. Crandall, "The Truth of a Toy," by Richard Schneider, "O Come Ye to Bethlehem," by Jeanette Doyle Parr, "To Have Christmas," by Dina Donahue, and "My Christmas Discovery," by Norman Vincent Peale reprinted from *The Guideposts Family Christmas Book*, © 1980 by Guideposts Associates, Inc., Carmel, New York, 10512. Used by permission. "An Advent Prayer," by Terri Castillo, "O Little Town," by Nancy Schraffenberger, "The Chicken-Pox Christmas," by Janet Martin, "The Miraculous Staircase," by Arthur Gordon, "Mrs. Pine's Happiest Christmas," by Robert Juhren, "The Christmas Rose," by Velma Seawell Daniels, "A Tree for Min," by Deborah Grandinetti, "The Christmas Doll," by Pat Sullivan, and "The Christmas No Gifts Came," by Drue Duke reprinted from *The Gifts of Christmas*, © 1981 by Guideposts Associates, Inc., Carmel, New York 10512. Used by permission. "A Christmas Tree—for the Birds, Too!," by June Masters Bacher, "A Lasting Christmas," by Garnett Ann Schultz, "Integrating the Family Treasures," by Ruth C. Ikerman, "A Pre-Christmas Prayer," by Drue Duke, "A Christmas List," by Marilyn Morgan Helleberg, "Surprise Packages," by Shirley Climo, "Look-Ahead Gifts," by June Masters Bacher, "The Christmas Miracle," by Jean Bell Mosley, "The Scarlet Robe," by Ann B. Benjamin, "The Christmas Eve I Smelled the Hay," by Marjorie Holmes, "This Day," by Rosalyn Hart Finch, "The Glory of Christmas," by Laverne Riley O'Brien, "The Donkey," by Van Varner, "The Best Shine in Peru," by James McDermott, "A Tradition All Her Own," by Frances E. Wilson, "Thank You, God," by Donna Russell, "The Littlest Camel," by Shirley Climo, "The Crooked Dogwood Tree," by Peggy Brooke, "Christmas-Like Hearts," by June Masters Bacher, "The Tie Clip," by Dick Schneider, and "Chrissy's Shell Tree," by Velma Seawell Daniels reprinted from *The Treasures of Christmas*, copyright © 1982 by Guideposts Associates, Inc., Carmel, New York 10512. Used by permission. "The Secret of Happy Giving," by Catherine Marshall, reprinted from *Guideposts* Magazine. Copyright © 1974 by Guideposts Associates, Inc., Carmel, New York 10512. "How to Make a Jesus Tree," reprinted from *Guideposts* Magazine. Copyright © 1976 by Guideposts Associates, Inc., Carmel, New York 10512. "Why Don't We—At Christmas?" reprinted from *Guideposts* Magazine. Copyright © 1979 by Guideposts Associates, Inc., Carmel, New York 10512. "Silent Night," by Elizabeth Sherrill," reprinted from *Guideposts* Magazine. Copyright © 1981 by Guideposts Associates, Inc., Carmel, New York, 10512. "Bring Us Together," by Marjorie Holmes, reprinted from *I've Got to Talk to Somebody, God*. Copyright © 1968, 1969 by Marjorie Holmes Mighell. Reprinted by permission of Doubleday & Co., Inc.